D1716044

Latino-American History

Spanish Settlement in North America

1822–1898

Latino-American History

Latino-American History

Spanish Settlement in North America

1822–1898

by Matthew Kachur and Jon Sterngass

Mark Overmyer-Velázquez, Ph.D., Consulting Editor

CHELSEA HOUSE PUBLISHERS
An imprint of Infobase Publishing

COVER *The Battle of Chapultepec in 1847 was one of many battles in the Mexican-American War.*

Spanish Settlement in North America

Copyright ©2007 by Infobase Publishing

For information contact:

Chelsea House
An imprint of Infobase Publishing
132 West 31st Street
New York, NY 10001

Library of Congress Cataloging-in-Publication Data
Kachur, Matthew.
    Spanish Settlement in North America / Matthew Kachur and Jon Sterngass.
        p. cm. — (Latino American history)
    Includes bibliographical references and index.
    ISBN 0-8160-6442-3 (hardcover)
    1. Southwest, New—History—to 1848—Juvenile literature. 2. Spaniards—United States—History—Juvenile literature. 3. United States—Foreign relations—Caribbean Area—Juvenile literature. 4. Caribbean Area—Foreign relations—United States—Juvenile literature. 5. Caribbean Area—History—1810-1945—Juvenile literature. 6. United States—Civilization—Spanish influences—Juvenile literature. I. Sterngass, Jon. II. Title. III. Series.
    F799.K37 2006
    979—dc22
2006017144

Chelsea House books are available at special discounts when purchased in bulk quantities for businesses, associations, institutions, or sales promotions. Please call our Special Sales Department in New York at (212) 967–8800 or (800) 322–8755.

You can find Chelsea House on the World Wide Web at **http://www.chelseahouse.com**

Cover design by Takeshi Takehashi

A Creative Media Applications Production
Interior design: Fabia Wargin & Luis Leon
Editor: Matt Levine
Copy editor: Laurie Lieb

Photo Credits
© Library of Congress, Washington, D.C., USA/The Bridgeman Art Library page: cover; New York Public Library, Astor, Lenox and Tilden Foundations pages: vi, 12, 30, 47, 74, 86, 77, 95; Courtesy of University of Southern California on behalf of the USC Specialized Libraries and Archival Collections page: 8; The Granger Collection, New York, pages: 16, 40, 68, 91; North Wind Picture Archives pages: 20, 22, 32, 53, 54, 64, 79; Private Collection/Peter Newark American Pictures/The Bridgeman Art Library page: 38; Courtesy of Palace of Governors pages: 42, 58; © Musee de l'Armee, Brussels, Belgium, Patrick Lorette/The Bridgeman Art Library page: 50; © Bibliotheque Nationale, Paris, France/Archives Charmet/The Bridgeman Art Library page: 88

Maps: Created by Ortelius Design

Printed in the United States of America

Bang CMA _____ _____ 10 9 8 7 6 5 4 3 2 1

This book is printed on acid-free paper.

Contents

Preface to the Series

by Mark Overmyer-Velázquez, Ph.D.,
Consulting Editor

"With all due respect to Uncle Sam, this [march] shows that Los Angeles has never stopped belonging to Mexico." This statement by Alberto Tinoco, a television reporter in Mexico, refers to the demonstration in support of immigrants that took place in Los Angeles, California, on March 25, 2006. An estimated 1 million people attended this march—mainly Mexicans and other Latinos. But does Los Angeles belong to Mexico? And what was so important that so many people came out to show their support for Latino immigrants?

The *Latino American History* series looks to answer these questions and many others. Los Angeles did belong to Mexico until 1848. At that time, Los Angeles and much of what is now called the American Southwest became part of the United States as a result of the Mexican-American War. Today, the enormous city, like many other places through-out the United States, is home to millions of Latinos.

The immigrant march made perfectly clear that people of Latin American descent have a historical power and presence in the United States. Latino history is central to

OPPOSITE A Spanish overlord supervises slaves harvesting sugarcane on a Caribbean plantation in the 1700s.

the history of the United States. Latinos have been closely connected to most regions in the United States in every era, from the 16th-century Spanish settlements in Florida and California to the contemporary surge of Latino populations in North Carolina, South Carolina, Oklahoma, Minnesota, and Connecticut.

The 2000 U.S. Census made Latinos' importance even plainer. Every 10 years, the government makes a survey of the country's population, called a census. The 2000 survey determined that, for the first time, Latinos outnumbered African Americans as the second-largest nonwhite population.

One of every seven people in the nation identifies himself or herself as Latino. This ethnic group has accounted for about half the growth in the U.S. population since 1990. There are over 41 million people of Latin American and Caribbean origins in the United States. Their presence will have a large impact on the futures of both the United States and Latin America.

Who Is Latino?

The term *Latino* emerged in the 1970s. It refers—somewhat loosely—to people, either male or female, living in the United States who have at least one parent of Latin American descent. The term is often used in contrast to terms such as *Anglo American, African American,* and *Asian American.* Most frequently, *Latino* refers to immigrants (and their descendants) who originally came to the United States from the Spanish-speaking countries of North, Central, and South America, as well as from countries in the Caribbean. This definition usually does not include Brazil, Haiti, and Belize, where the chief language is not Spanish, but does include Puerto Rico, which is a U.S. territory.

The other popular term to describe this population, *Hispanic,* was developed by the U.S. government in the 1970s as a way to categorize people of Latin American descent. However, Latinos consider this label to wrongly identify them more with Spain than with Latin America. In addition, most Latinos first identify with their own national or subnational (state, city, or village) origins. For example, a woman with roots in the Dominican Republic might first identify herself as *una dominicana* and then as a Latina. The word *Latino* causes further confusion when discussing the thousands of non–Spanish-speaking American Indians who have immigrated to the United States from Latin America.

Four main factors over time have determined the presence of Latinos in the United States. They are U.S. military and economic involvement in Latin America, relaxed immigration laws for entry into the United States, population growth in Latin America, and wages that were higher in the United States than in Latin America. These factors have shaped the patterns of migration to the United States since the mid-19th century.

"We Didn't Cross the Border, the Border Crossed Us"   1848

Many Mexicans still call the Mexican-American War from 1846 to 1848 the "North American Invasion." In the first decades of the 19th century, Mexico's economy and military were weak from years of fighting. There had been a war for independence from Spain followed by a series of civil wars among its own people. During the same period, the United States was eager to expand its borders. It looked to Mexico for new land. The war cost Mexico almost half its territory, including what would become the U.S. states of California, Nevada, Arizona, New Mexico, and Texas. Some Mexican citizens left on the U.S. side of the new border proclaimed, "We didn't cross the border, the border crossed us."

The territory that had belonged to Mexico brought new citizens of Mexican background to the United States, as well as enormous mineral and land wealth. Consider the famous gold rush that started in 1848 on former Mexican territory in California. That event and the vast expanse of farmlands and pasture lands once belonging to Mexico were vital to the westward expansion of the United States. Mexicans on the north side of the new border became U.S. citizens and the country's first Latinos. As the West became industrialized and demand for labor grew, it was often migrant Mexican workers who labored in the fields and factories of the prospering economy.

1898   The Spanish-American War, Puerto Rico, and the Harvest of Empire

The term *harvest of empire* refers to the arrival of Latino immigrants in the United States as a direct result of U.S. military involvement in Latin America, starting with Mexico in 1848. The United States created political and economic uncertainty through the use of force and the support of dictatorships in the "garden" of Latin America. Then the United States harvested the resulting millions of homeless and jobless Latinos. The United States's harvest of empire peaked with the 1898 Spanish-American War.

> **Fast Fact**
>
> American Indians who have migrated to the United States may identify themselves with a small village or perhaps a state of origin. For example, Zapoteco immigrants from the state of Oaxaca, Mexico, have developed Oaxacan hometown associations in Los Angeles and other U.S. cities.

The U.S. military freed the island of Puerto Rico from Spanish colonial rule in 1898. The island's residents never would have imagined that they would be colonized yet again, this time by the United States. The island became a U.S. territory. The U.S. president had the power to choose the governor and other high-level administrators. In 1917, Congress made all Puerto Ricans U.S. citizens.

In the 1950s, Puerto Rico suffered economic problems and joblessness. Immigration to the United States rapidly expanded, resulting in the largest movement of Latin Americans to the United States in history. New laws in the 1960s only increased Latin American immigration to the United States.

The Hart-Celler Act and Recent Latino Migration

1965

On October 3, 1965, President Lyndon Johnson signed the Hart-Celler Act, introducing a new era of mass immigration. The act made people's work skills and their need to unite with their families the most important elements in deciding who could immigrate to the United States. The new legislation eventually ended a system that used people's countries of origin to decide the number of immigrants who were allowed into the United States. The Hart-Celler Act supposedly put people of all nations on an equal footing to immigrate to the United States. The act created the foundation for today's immigration laws.

Between 1960 and 2000, Latin America's population skyrocketed from 218 million to over 520 million. Political instability in the region, in addition to this growing population, meant increased needs for migration and work. Many people turned to the economic opportunities of the United States as a strategy for survival.

At the same time, in the United States, agricultural, industrial, and domestic employers depended upon the ability to pay immigrant laborers from Latin America lower wages. As a result, Latino labor has almost always been welcomed in the United States, despite the government's repeated attempts to restrict immigration in the past century. The demands of U.S. employers for Latino immigrant labor have always shaped the tone of the immigration debate.

Fast Fact

In 1960, 75 percent of the foreign-born population of the United States came from Europe. Only 14 percent came from Latin America and Asia. As a result of the Hart-Celler Act, by 2000, only 15 percent of immigrants were European and more than 77 percent were Latin American and Asian. This trend promises to continue.

Many Latino Histories

The events of the years 1848, 1898, and 1965 explain how and why Latinos migrated to the United States. However, these events do not reveal much about what happened once the Latinos arrived. Despite their many shared experiences, Latinos are anything but an easily defined people. Although television and film have tended to portray all Latinos as similar, they come from a wide range of national, ethnic, social, economic, and political backgrounds, which have divided as much as united this growing population. Such backgrounds include "African," "Anglo," "Asian," "Indian," and any combinations of these.

Mexicans started migrating to the United States in the 19th century and Puerto Ricans in the early 20th century. Immigrants from Chile, Argentina, El Salvador, Guatemala, and other South and Central American countries made their way north in large numbers starting in the 1960s. Many of these Latinos were seeking shelter from brutal military dictatorships. Once in the United States, Latinos of all backgrounds have continued to mix with each other and with local populations, forging a whole new set of identities. Latino communities keep and develop their own cultures in new and creative ways in the United States, adding to the rich diversity of the country.

Indeed, Latinos have contributed to U.S. society in other ways besides their investments in the country's economy and labor. In politics, education, sports, and the arts, Latinos are a growing presence. By exploring the origins and development of U.S. Latinos, this series, *Latino American History*, helps us to better understand how our Latin American neighbors to the south have become our Latino neighbors next door.

Introduction

When the United States took over the Spanish colony of Florida in 1821, the people who lived in that area suddenly became U.S. residents. In 1836, the Spanish-speaking people of Texas woke up one morning as citizens of the independent Republic of Texas. In 1845, the same people found themselves in the state of Texas and part of the United States of America. In 1848, Latinos in what was northern Mexico—California, Arizona, Colorado, and New Mexico—joined the United States without having been asked if they wanted to switch countries. Finally, in 1898, the United States took over Puerto Rico and made it a U.S. territory without consulting the citizens of this Caribbean island.

These Latinos did not choose to leave their homelands and come to the United States. Instead, the United States came to them. An old Tejano expression says, "We didn't cross the border, the border crossed us." (A Tejano is a Texan of Mexican descent.) This is the main story of Latinos in the United States in the 1800s. In general, Latino immigrants did not pour into the United States in the 19th century, as did immigrants from Europe. Instead, the border came to them, whether they liked it or not.

OPPOSITE   Antonio Coronel and his wife outside their home in Los Angeles, California. Coronel become mayor of Los Angeles in 1853.

Latino Americans Seek Independence

The story of Spanish settlement in North America begins with Spanish settlement in South America, Central America, Mexico, and the Caribbean. The decline of this Spanish empire in the 1800s had an enormous impact on U.S. history. Rebellions against the Spanish, especially in Mexico and Cuba, would eventually lead to U.S. involvement in these battles and the presence of thousands of Spanish-speaking people in the United States.

From the 1500s to the early 1800s, the monarchs of Spain controlled all of South America except Brazil and some isolated lands in the north. After the American Revolution (1775–1783) and the French Revolution (1789–1799), however, many Latinos in the Americas began to believe in the ideals of equality and human rights. They hoped to establish democratic governments.

After 300 years of Spanish rule, many Latino Americans considered themselves very different from their Spanish rulers. They believed that they had developed a new culture and ways of thought that were different from those of Spain. They believed that only people who had spent a lifetime in the Americas could properly understand their needs.

Mexico and the United States

Spain's largest territory in America was Mexico. When Mexico became independent from Spain in 1821, it included the entire present-day states of Texas, California, New Mexico, Arizona, Colorado, and Utah. These northern areas represented almost 40 percent of Mexico's territory. The independence of Mexico had a great effect on the United States because the two countries share a common boundary. Over the next 80 years, Mexico's northern lands would be the center of many disputes between Mexico and the United States. In the end, Mexico would be forced to surrender much of its northern territory to the United States.

Florida, Cuba, and the Caribbean

Cuba is only 90 miles (145 km) away from the North American mainland. After Spain invaded Cuba in the 1490s, it was only a short trip for Spanish explorers to sail to Florida and create a colony in 1565. The United States took over the Spanish colony of Florida in 1821. As the 19th century progressed, the United States would become more and more involved in the politics and economy of the Caribbean Islands. These islands produced much of the world's sugar, coffee, and other important crops. Large U.S. companies would influence U.S. relations and policy toward the Caribbean Islands. Many Latinos from the Caribbean settled in the United States and contributed to the diversity of Latino culture in America.

The involvement of the United States with Latino peoples in the former Spanish territories would have a lasting impact on the history of the Americans. In addition, the roles and influence of Latino Americans in the United States would grow dramatically during 19th century.

Californios and Tejanos

1

Spanish settlers first came to California in 1769, when the Spanish in New Spain established a Catholic mission at San Diego. A mission was a settlement where Christianity was preached for the first time in an area where there were no native priests. By 1823, a string of 20 missions stretched along the California coast from San Diego to Sonoma. The Spanish built the missions to try to win over American Indians to the Christian religion. These missions owned millions of acres of land in California.

Settlements grew up around these missions. In these communities, Spanish colonists and Indian laborers grew wheat and corn and raised livestock. Settlers also lived outside the missions in little towns called pueblos. Another type of Spanish settlement was the presidio, or fort. At presidios, Spanish soldiers fought off American Indians and made sure the Spanish government held onto the land it claimed. In general, the Latino settlers hugged the Pacific coast of California. Very few settled in the California interior.

In 1820, the Spanish population of California numbered less than 5,000. These people were called Californios. They

OPPOSITE This image of San Francisco, which was originally named Yerba Buena, shows the city as it looked in 1846 before the discovery of gold in California.

were Spanish-speaking people who had come from New Spain or Spain to settle in California. California was far from the center of Mexican population and government around Mexico City. The Spanish government appointed government officials for California but generally left the area alone. Therefore, Californios developed a culture of their own.

Although lured to California by rumors of gold and silver deposits there, the Spanish discovered very little gold and silver in California. Instead, Spanish-speaking settlers became farmers, ranchers, or laborers. Raising cattle became a very important occupation. Government officials, priests, soldiers, and skilled craftspeople settled in towns, missions, and presidios.

The Age of the Rancho

In 1821, New Spain won its independence from Spain. The area was now known as Mexico. In the 1830s, the Mexican congress passed laws taking away the land that belonged to the Catholic missions in California. The Mexican government in turn divided this land and sold it or gave it away. Some Californios gained great stretches of this former mission property and established huge ranchos (ranches) along the coast. By 1846, the Mexican government had made about 800 land grants totaling almost 9 million acres (3.6 million ha). Most Mexicans in California owned and managed small family farms. In fact, less than 5 percent of California's Mexican population could be considered rancheros (ranch owners). It was the large ranchos, however, that made Californio life distinctive.

Californio ranchers sold cow-hides and tallow, an animal fat used to make candles and soap. These were California's only important trade items. The cowhides were in great demand in the United States. A visitor to southern California in the 1830s wrote that "the desolate-look-ing place we were in furnished more hides than any port on the coast . . . about thirty miles [48 km] in the interior was a fine plain country, filled with herds of cattle, in the center of which was the Pueblo de Los Angeles—the largest town in California." Confirming this account, Juan Ramon Pico, the nephew of California's last Spanish governor, wrote,

> *There was no business in the country then but the raising of cattle. All summer long the cows fed over the oat covered hills in the mornings and mowed away the clover into their four stomachs during the afternoon. . . . By November each one was as fat as [it] could get and yet manage to walk. The vaqueros [cowboys] and Los Indos came many days journey across the San Joaquin Valley, driving big herds of cattle to be killed for hides and tallow.*

It was not hard to get a land grant from the Mexican government. All a person needed was proof of Mexican citi-zenship, a *diseño* (map) showing the approximate bound-aries of the rancho, and a willingness to live in a ranch house and provide the cattle. No payment was required.

Fast Fact

The ranchos of the Californios became enormous. By 1850, about 200 Californio families owned about 14 million acres (5.7 million ha) of California land.

As a result, large ranchos flourished in Mexican California. For example, in 1844, Pío and Andrés Pico owned a 130,000-acre (53,000-ha) ranch that reached 20 miles (32 km) from present-day Oceanside to the present-day Orange County line near San Clemente and east to the foothills and coastal mountains. The grand rancho of the Peralta family included the area now covered by Berkeley, Oakland, Alameda, and part of the Santa Clara Valley. The Peralta ranch had its own chapel, bullring, private dock, and fleet of barges to transport goods on San Francisco Bay. Most ranchos were self-sufficient; they produced almost everything they needed.

This engraving of Andrés Pico shows the California rancher and soldier as he looked in the mid–1800s.

Large ranchos were not limited to people who were Mexican citizens by birth. A person might marry into an old Californio family, pay a $20 fee to become a Catholic, swear allegiance to Mexico, and become a ranchero. For example, Henry Delano Fitch, a U.S. sea captain, married Josefa Carrillo, a daughter of wealthy Californio rancher Joaquín Carrillo, and became a powerful landowner in his own right. Many of the most important men from the United States who settled in Mexican California achieved power, influence, and Mexican citizenship by marrying *una hija del pais* (a daughter of the land).

Some U.S. residents became rich in California without the benefit of such a marriage. John Sutter, for example, was born in Germany to Swiss parents. He immigrated to the United States in 1834 and operated as a trader on the Santa Fe Trail. In 1839, he moved to California. The Mexican government granted him nearly 50,000 acres (20,000 ha) to establish a settlement east of San Francisco (then called Yerba Buena) along the Sacramento River. Within a few years, Sutter had become a wealthy landowner with a herd of 13,000 cattle.

These wealthy Californios enjoyed a life of ease and pleasure, attending fiestas, watching bullfights, and betting on horse races. Rich Californios tried to show off their wealth. John Bidwell, who became an important California politician, immigrated to Mexican California in 1841. He wrote, "They had a custom of never charging for anything . . . for entertainment, food, use of horses, etc." However, the lifestyle of these wealthy Californios was built on the backs of vast numbers of Indians who

The Myth of "Spanish" California

In the 1880s, nostalgic Californios and some Anglos (white non-Spanish speakers) in the United States created the myth of "Spanish California." According to this fantasy, California in the early 1800s was not "Mexican" but "Spanish," filled with courteous rancheros, fabulous fiestas, helpful missions, and almost no mesti-zos or Indians. In 1890, a Californio named Guadalupe Vallejo helped spread this myth. Vallejo wrote:

> It seems to me that there never was a more peaceful or happy people . . . than the Spanish, Mexican, and Indian population of Alta California before the American conquest. . . . The houses of the Spanish people were . . . very comfortable, cool in summer and warm in winter. . . . There was much gaiety and social life, even though people were widely scattered.

did the hard labor on the ranchos and poor Californio ranch hands who maintained the herds of cattle. These workers labored under very harsh conditions.

Richard Henry Dana Visits California

In 1834, Richard Henry Dana worked as a sailor on a ship bound for the California coast. In 1836, he wrote *Two Years before the Mast*, a classic sailing story. In the book, he described trade in Monterey:

> The Californians . . . can make nothing for themselves. The country abounds in grapes, yet they buy, at a great price, bad wine made in Boston and brought round by us. . . . Their hides, too, which they value at two dollars in money, they barter for something which costs seventy-five cents in Boston. . . . Things sell, on an average, at an advance of nearly three hundred per cent upon the Boston prices.

Trade with the United States

The Spanish had tried to force Californians to trade only with Spain or its colonies. California's settlers and traders could reach central Mexico only by long overland journeys or tricky sea voyages down the Pacific coast. However, Mexican independence in 1821 opened California to trade with other countries, especially the United States. In the 1820s, sailing ships from the east coast of the United States traveled around Cape Horn at the southern tip of South America and up to the California coast. Ships brought manufactured goods from the United States and England and returned with hides and tallow from California.

Overland travel routes linking California to the United States also increased the possibilities of trade. The Old Spanish Trail, established in 1829, ran from Los Angeles to Santa

Fe, the largest Mexican settlement west of the Mississippi, in the Mexican province of New Mexico. In Santa Fe, the Old Spanish Trail connected to the 800-mile (1,300-km) path known as the Santa Fe Trail. The Santa Fe Trail linked New Mexico and the United States.

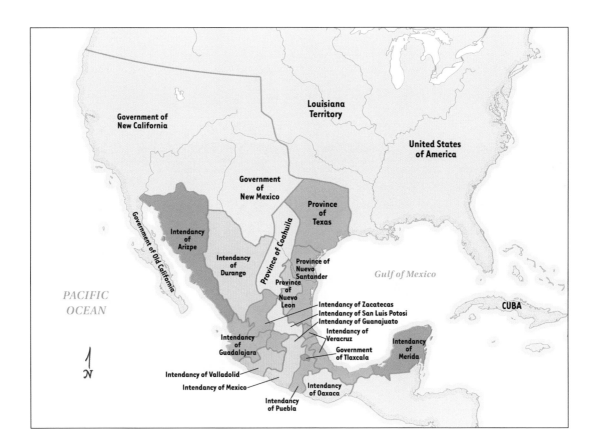

Government of New California

Louisiana Territory

United States of America

Government of New Mexico

Province of Texas

Government of Old California

Province of Coahuila

Intendancy of Arizpe

Intendancy of Durango

Province of Nuevo Santander

Gulf of Mexico

Province of Nuevo Leon

Intendancy of Zacatecas
Intendancy of San Luis Potosi
Intendancy of Guanajuato
Intendancy of Veracruz

PACIFIC OCEAN

CUBA

Intendancy of Guadalajara

Government of Tlaxcala

Intendancy of Merida

Intendancy of Valladolid
Intendancy of Mexico

Intendancy of Oaxaca

Intendancy of Puebla

N

This map of Mexico shows how the country was divided about 1821.

Between 1821 and 1846, Anglo-Americans began to trickle into California. In 1826, Captain Jedediah Smith and his party of hunters and trappers became the first large group from the United States to travel overland across the continent to California. New England whaling ships began to stop at California ports. Other U.S. merchant ships appeared on the coast to buy sea otter and seal furs for trade in China. Boston merchants sent vessels to trade for cattle hides and tallow. A few mountain men searching for beaver crossed the Sierra Nevada into northern California. Gradually people in California and New Mexico began feeling closer to the United States than to Mexico.

A Spanish family travels by oxcart to California in the 1800s.

The Colonization of Texas

The province of Texas was far from California, but the story of its Latino settlement was somewhat similar. European Spaniards and their descendants dominated Texas from the 1500s until the mid-1800s. The Spanish came to present-day Texas and Arizona (known as Pimería Alta under the

Spanish) in search of gold and silver. However, it quickly became apparent that Texas was not as rich in mineral wealth as central Mexico or Peru.

The Spanish tried to use the same mission and presidio system in Texas that they used in California. However, for most of the Spanish period, settlers in Texas and Arizona lived in fear of raids by warlike Native American tribes like the Comanche, who fought to hold onto their rich buffalo lands. Spanish efforts resulted in only a few permanent settlements in Texas and Arizona. The main Spanish settlements, such as Goliad and San Antonio, were small and far apart.

Like California, Texas under Spanish—and then Mexican—rule became known as a cattle-raising province. Ranchers raised large and profitable herds. They would drive the cattle to market to the south in Mexico or to the east in Louisiana. There were also scatterings of small farmers and common laborers.

When Mexico became independent in 1821, Texas became part of the Mexican state of Coahuila y Tejas. At that time, there were only about 4,000 Spanish-speaking settlers in Texas. Most of them were natives of Mexico or born in Texas. The road to Mexico City was rough and difficult. Tejanos did not look to central Mexico for much more than weapons, gunpowder, and cloth.

Tejanos and Californios were tough, independent, and self-sufficient. They created small but successful colonies in northern Mexico. In the 1820s, however, this frontier culture was suddenly faced with competition from Anglo immigrants from the United States. The winner would be the dominant force on the North American continent.

The Texas Revolt

2

During the 1800s many people in the United States believed that God wanted the United States to expand its territory across the entire continent. This idea was known as manifest destiny. The population of the country nearly doubled between 1820 and 1840. U.S. citizens claimed they needed more land. At times, supporters of manifest destiny encouraged the United States to take over Canada, Mexico, the Caribbean, and Central America.

U.S. citizens wanted to believe that the conquest of western North America was an attempt to extend liberty and progress. They did not want to admit it was also based on a desire for other people's land. Advances in transportation, communication, and industry had convinced many citizens that the United States was a special nation and that white North Americans were a superior race. These expansionists proclaimed that only English-speaking Anglo-Saxons had the energy and love of liberty to establish democratic governments. White U.S. citizens who promoted the idea of manifest destiny therefore looked down on American Indians, African Americans, and Mexicans and thought that these so-called inferior groups

OPPOSITE Mexican troops overwhelm the Texans inside the Alamo during the famous battle for Texas independence in 1836.

had to be controlled, moved out of the way, or even killed. Although it is hard to respect the idea of manifest destiny in the 21st century, it was a strongly held belief in the United States in the 1800s.

Anglos in Spanish Texas

Any expansion of the United States to the west would bring it into conflict with Mexico. When Mexico won its independence from Spain in 1821, the new nation was very large. Mexico's northern provinces were far from the center of Mexican population around Mexico City. Only about 4,000 Spanish-speaking residents lived in Texas and 4,000 more in California. New Mexico, with about 36,000 Spanish-speaking residents, was by far the largest Spanish-speaking settlement in Mexico's northern provinces in 1821.

Mexico tried to strengthen its border areas by increasing their population. To encourage citizens of the United States to settle in Texas, Mexico offered land almost free of charge to U.S. *empresarios* (land agents). In exchange, the empresarios had to agree to become Mexican citizens, adopt the Catholic religion, and bring 200 families to Texas.

Moses Austin and his son Stephen received a land grant in 1821 covering almost 18,000 acres (7,300 ha). Twenty-five other U.S. settlements quickly followed in east and central Texas. By 1835, about 35,000 people from the United States (including 2,000 slaves) lived in Mexican Texas. U.S. settlers outnumbered Mexicans in Texas at least three to one and maybe as much as ten to one.

The Texans Revolt

Most whites in Texas never wanted to be part of Mexico. They argued with local Mexicans over land titles, complained about local laws, owned black slaves (slavery was illegal in Mexico), and constantly asserted the inferiority of Mexicans.

In 1835, the U.S. citizens in Texas, joined by a few local Latinos, began a revolt against the government of Mexico. Stephen Austin and a force of 500 Texans attacked San Antonio and conquered the presidio known as the Alamo. Mexican general Antonio López de Santa Anna hurried north with an army of 6,000 men to crush the rebellion. When the Mexican army approached San Antonio in February 1836, less than 200 Texans held the Alamo. After a two-week siege, the Mexicans stormed the Alamo and captured it. All the defenders were killed, including well-known frontiersmen Jim Bowie and Davy Crockett.

In March, Santa Anna ordered the execution of prisoners of war who were taken after a battle near Goliad. However, Santa Anna's use of harsh warfare backfired. Texans quickly

Slavery in Texas

People in the United States sometimes claim that the Texans revolted for "freedom." However, Mexican rule of Texas had not been particularly harsh. Texans had done pretty much what they pleased. But many Texan Americans were white Southerners who owned slaves. Mexico's refusal to allow slavery was one of the Anglo settlers' main complaints that caused the rebellion.

When Texas declared its independence in 1836, it quickly adopted a constitution legalizing slavery. The region joined the United States as a slave state in 1845. Sixteen years later, during the U.S. Civil War, Texas seceded, or withdrew, from the United States in order to defend the right to own slaves.

Juan Seguín

Juan Seguín (1806–1890) was a founder of the Republic of Texas. He was born into a long-established Tejano family in San Antonio that was friends with Stephen Austin. Seguín led pro-independence Tejanos against the Mexican army in 1835 and 1836.

After Texas gained its independence from Mexico, the residents elected Seguín to the Texas senate in 1838 and then as mayor of San Antonio in 1840. However, anti-Latino Anglos forced him to resign as mayor and flee to Mexico in 1842.

Seguín later served in the Mexican army and fought in the Mexican-American War (1846–1848) against the United States. After the war, Seguín returned to Texas, but again Anglo racism forced him back to Mexico. In 1858, Seguín wrote his memoirs. His book was the first auto-biography by a Mexican American in English. He died in 1890 in Nuevo Laredo, just across the Rio Grande from Texas.

organized an army led by Sam Houston, a former governor of Tennessee. On April 21, Houston surprised and defeated a larger Mexican force at San Jacinto, near present-day Houston. The Texans captured Santa Anna and forced him to sign a treaty of independence, setting the boundary of the new Republic of Texas at the Rio Grande. The Mexican congress—and later Santa Anna himself—rejected this treaty. They claimed it was an agreement made under "threat of death." Therefore, Mexico did not recognize Texas's independence and did not accept that the boundary of the province was the Rio Grande.

Many Tejanos tried to stay neutral during this rebellion. A few stood with Anglo Texans in supporting independence. Tejanos died at the Alamo and served at San Jacinto. Juan Seguín, the most famous Tejano supporter of independence, was at the Alamo for the first part of the siege. He survived only because he left to gather reinforcements. Seguín later led a cavalry unit protecting Sam Houston's army.

The Lone Star Republic

Although Texas was now independent, the Anglos in charge wanted to join the United States. However, two major issues made the United States hesitate to annex, or lay claim to, Texas. First, Mexico absolutely opposed the move. The Mexican government stated several times that if the United States annexed Texas, war with Mexico would follow. Secondly, if Texas joined the United States, it would be as a state that permitted slavery. Most people in the northern United States did not support adding another slave state to the nation.

This left Texans no choice. They wrote a constitution for the Republic of Texas and nicknamed their new country the Lone Star Republic. Texas remained an independent nation for almost 10 years. During that time, its population soared from 30,000 to 142,000. Most of the new settlers came from the southern United States.

Mexicans in Texas faced a difficult position after the Texas revolt. Many Anglos hated everything connected with Mexico. Some towns in Texas, including San Antonio, tried to expel all their Tejano residents. Many Tejano families left for Mexico, but there were some important exceptions. José Antonio Navarro and Francisco Ruiz served in the congress of the Republic of Texas. Antonio Menchaca was a mayor of San Antonio. Navarro, Ruiz, and Lorenzo de Zavala were signers of Texas's declaration of independence.

> **Fast Fact**
>
> In 1834, Lorenzo de Zavala wrote the first book of travel literature by a Latino traveling in the United States. Zavala later served as vice president of the Texas Republic. In 1836, he designed the first flag of Texas.

Texas Joins the United States

The election of 1844 was one of the closest in U.S. history. James Polk defeated Henry Clay by 38,000 votes out of 2.7 million votes cast. The new president was a slaveholding cotton grower from Tennessee and a strong believer in manifest destiny.

In early 1845, the U.S. Congress finally annexed Texas. The vote was only 27 to 25 in the Senate. The exact boundary of the new state of Texas was not clearly set.

The annexation of Texas led directly to the Mexican-American War. Massachusetts representative (and former president) John Quincy Adams wrote in his diary that the annexation of Texas was thus the "heaviest calamity that ever befell" the United States.

The Mexican-American War Begins

After President Polk took office, he declared that the Rio Grande was the southern border of Texas. The river lay far beyond what had been the southern boundary when Texas had been a Mexican province. The Mexicans claimed the border was the Nueces River, 130 miles (210 km) to the north and east of the Rio Grande.

In 1846, Polk ordered General Zachary Taylor to advance into the disputed territory between the two rivers. The Mexicans sent their own soldiers to the area. A fight broke out between the two armies in April. Polk asked for a declaration of war and the U.S. Congress agreed. The Mexican-American War was extremely popular in the United States, especially in the South. Many white Southerners hoped that slavery would spread into any newly conquered territories.

However, many U.S. citizens, including U.S. representative Abraham Lincoln, did not support the war. In 1846, the U.S. House of Representatives passed a resolution stating that the Mexican-American War was unconstitutional and unnecessary and blamed President Polk for starting it.

The War in California

The Mexican-American War was supposed to be about the border between Texas and Mexico. However, President Polk already had decided to take a great deal more of Mexican territory. As soon as the war broke out in 1846, Polk wrote in his diary that

> *if the war should be [a long one], it would in my judgment be very important that the US should hold military possession of California at the time peace was made, and I declared my purpose to be to acquire for the US, California, New Mexico, and perhaps some of the Northern Provinces of Mexico.*

In the 1840s, there were still fewer than 8,000 Mexicans of Spanish origin living in California. About 1,500 people from the United States lived there. Like the Anglo settlers in Texas, these U.S. immigrants had no loyalty to Mexico. In 1846, John C. Frémont and a few of these people organized a rebellion against Mexico. They declared California's independence and raised a flag picturing a bear. This "Bear Flag

U.S. general Stephen Kearney declared New Mexico part of the United States after his troops had taken the town of Santa Fe without firing a shot in 1846.

Republic" lasted only a month. After the Mexican-American War began, the U.S. Navy landed 250 sailors and marines in Monterey and declared California a part of the United States. In southern California, U.S. soldiers captured the towns of Santa Barbara, Los Angeles, and San Diego. By 1847, the entire province of California was in U.S. hands.

New Mexico

About 60,000 Mexicans lived in the Mexican province of New Mexico, and most did not want to join the United States. However, New Mexico stood directly in the path of U.S. expansion to California.

When the Mexican-American War began in 1846, General Stephen Kearney and an army of 1,700 men invaded Mexico's northern provinces. Kearney took Santa Fe without firing a shot. Declaring that New Mexico's residents were now U.S. citizens, he set up a temporary government and set off for California.

In January 1846, after Kearney left, Mexicans and American Indians began a rebellion known as the Taos Revolt. These long-time residents of New Mexico did not want to live under U.S. rule. For a while, the rebels resisted the U.S. soldiers sent to put down the revolt. However, by the end of 1847, U.S. forces had retaken complete control of New Mexico.

The Treaty of Guadalupe Hidalgo

U.S. forces won most of the battles of the Mexican-American War and soon occupied Mexico's northern provinces. Yet the Mexicans refused to give up. In 1847, General Winfield Scott and 14,000 U.S. soldiers landed at Veracruz in central Mexico. The troops then marched 260 miles (420 km) to the west and conquered Mexico City. The Mexicans finally agreed to peace.

The Mexican-American War ended with the Treaty of Guadalupe Hidalgo in 1848. The treaty gave Texas to the United States and set its boundary at the Rio Grande. Mexico also gave the provinces of California and New Mexico to the United States. These 1.2 million acres (486,000 ha) were 40 percent of Mexico's territory. The land increased the size of the United States by more than 20 percent. The U.S. government gave Mexico a payment of $15 million. The Treaty of Guadelupe Hidalgo completely reversed the balance of power on the North American continent.

The new U.S. territories contained about 150,000 American Indians and 100,000 Mexicans. Only about 2,000 people chose to return to Mexico. The rest decided to stay and became U.S. citizens.

Northerners and Southerners in the United States soon began to argue over whether slavery should be permitted in the new territories acquired from Mexico. In this way, the Mexican-American War became one of the indirect causes of the U.S. Civil War, which began only 12 years later.

The Decline
of the Californios

3

The Treaty of Guadalupe Hidalgo turned Californios into U.S. citizens. The treaty supposedly guaranteed them the rights to their lands. These rights, however, would soon be weakened.

In January 1848, James Marshall discovered gold at John Sutter's mill on the American River in the Sierra Nevada. This discovery occurred only one month before Mexico transferred California to the United States. On March 15, 1848, a San Francisco newspaper printed the first story about the discovery of gold. Only two weeks later, the paper had to shut down because its entire staff had left their jobs to hunt for gold. In its last edition, the paper wrote, "The whole country, from San Francisco to Los Angeles . . . resounds with the sordid cry of Gold! Gold! Gold! while the field is left half-planted, the house half-built, and everything neglected but the manufacture of shovels and pickaxes."

The years of 1849 and 1850 were the time of the California gold rush, when people rushed to the area where gold had been discovered. In 1845, about 1,000 Anglo

OPPOSITE Mexican vaqueros, or cowboys, like the one in this engraving, worked on rancheros throughout northern Mexico. This area included the territories that would become the states of California, New Mexico, Arizona, Texas, Utah, and Colorado.

Americans lived in California. In 1850, more than 100,000 Anglo Americans lived in California. San Francisco exploded from a village of 1,000 people in 1848 to 35,000 in 1850. California became the 31st state of the United States in 1850. By 1852, about 250,000 miners from around the world had arrived in California. About 25,000 of these immigrants came from Sonora and other Mexican states.

In 1859, Richard Henry Dana returned to California. He wrote,

> *When I . . . looked from my windows over the city of San Francisco, with its storehouses, towers, and steeples; its courthouses, theaters, and hospitals . . . its wharves and harbor, with their thousand-ton [900-mt] clipper ships . . . when I saw all these things and reflected on what I once . . . saw here . . . I could scarcely keep my hold of reality.*

The discovery of gold in California was a disaster for the Californios. After the gold rush, the non-Indian, Spanish-speaking population of California fell from about 70 percent in 1846 to 15 percent by 1850 and to 4 percent by 1870. Most U.S. citizens considered Californios "foreigners" even though they had lived on their lands for generations.

Discrimination

Anglos and Mexican Americans had used stereotypes to describe each other since the 1500s. Anglos believed that Mexicans were lazy, sneaky, dishonest, and controlled by

Catholic priests. Anglo writers usually described Spanish-speaking women as immoral. Mexicans regarded Anglos as arrogant, cruel, and greedy.

Anglos knew that most Mexicans were at least partly descended from American Indians. Most people in the United States considered American Indians an inferior race, and they carried over this prejudice to Mexicans and Mexican Americans. In spite of this discrimination, Mexicans and Mexican Americans took pride in their community. They believed that their history and experience set them apart from the Anglos who now controlled the area.

Loss of Political Power

Californios took part in the California government after the U.S. conquest. In 1849, eight of the forty-eight delegates who wrote the state's constitution were Mexican Americans. In 1851, Los Angeles city officials passed the first school law supporting bilingual education. In some places in southern California, away from the gold mines, Californios even remained a majority until the 1880s. However, in most of California, the flood of Anglo immigrants quickly reduced Mexican-American political power to almost nothing.

Immigrants to California in the 1850s included miners from Chile, Peru, and the Mexican province of Sonora. One Mexican noted that Sonorans "were accustomed to prospecting and . . . consequently achieved quicker, greater results" than Anglos. The Mexicans' success made Anglo miners furious. One Anglo prospector stated that Mexicans "had no business . . . to come to the land that god had given us. And if he was a native Californian, or 'greaser,' then so much the worse for him . . . we hated his whole degenerate thieving, landowning, lazy, discontented race."

In 1850, the California legislature passed the Foreign Miners' Tax Law to eliminate Mexican competition in the mines. The law stated that "foreign" miners had to pay $20 a month (equivalent to about $360 today) if they wanted to search for gold in California. This law applied not only to foreign immigrants but also to California-born Mexicans, who had supposedly become U.S. citizens under the Treaty of Guadalupe Hidalgo. Other laws discriminating against Mexicans quickly followed.

In addition to legal discrimination, Mexicans faced violence. Anglo mobs shot and lynched Latinos, murdering them without a lawful trial. Anglos also squatted on, or illegally occupied, Mexican-American land. Anti-Mexican prejudice spread throughout northern California, convincing most Mexicans that the region was not a place where they wanted to live.

Loss of Land

Mexican Americans had a difficult time keeping their property as the flood of Anglos grew. Some greedy miners squatted on Latino ranches without the permission of the landowners. Sometimes, squatters seized land violently, killing cattle, burning crops, and chasing Californios out of their homes.

Other Anglos used the law courts to make unfair claims on Californio property. The Land Act of 1851 set up a three-member Board of Land Commissioners to review the land rights of Californios. When a new settler claimed a Californio's land, the two parties would take the argument to a local court. If the verdict was appealed, the case moved to a U.S. district court and then the Supreme Court. Of 813 claims, 549 were appealed, some as many as six times. The California Board of Land Commissioners stopped functioning in 1856, but the seemingly endless appeals of their decisions caused land cases to drag on for an average of 17 years.

Rancheros had a difficult time proving they owned their land. Many of them had only carelessly drawn titles and maps from another time. The fact that they had been living on the land for decades meant nothing. Even though most Californios managed to prove ownership, the years of legal fees and court costs forced many to sell the land they had fought to save. By 1860, more than 80 percent of the Spanish-speaking residents of old northern Mexico had lost their lands.

Latinos in the Civil War

When the U.S. Civil War broke out, many Latinos considered it an Anglo issue and took a neutral position. Yet some Mexican Americans saw service in the military as a way to stake their claim as "true" citizens of the United States. Estimates of the number of Latinos who fought in this bloody war range from a few thousand to 20,000. Most of these soldiers came from New Mexico. The First Battalion of Native Cavalry was formed to take advantage of the superb horsemanship of the Mexican Americans of California.

In the New Mexico Territory, Latinos played a crucial role in turning back a Confederate invasion from Texas in 1862. At Glorieta Pass near Santa Fe, Latino soldiers from Colorado advanced behind the Confederate lines and destroyed the Southern supply train. This success forced the Confederates to retreat and freed New Mexico from Southern control.

The Mysterious Joaquín Murieta

This image of Joaquín Murieta shows the legendary bandit and folk hero as he looked about 1850.

One Californio who refused to accept the new Anglo rule peacefully was Joaquín Murieta, a legendary figure in California's Calaveras County in the 1850s. Murieta was either a bloodthirsty bandit or a Latino patriot, depending on one's point of view. It could be that the adventures of several bandits in the region were attributed to one "Joaquín." At this date, it is almost impossible to separate fact from legend.

Joaquín Murieta was supposedly born in 1829. He immigrated to California in 1850, but he met with only racism and discrimination. According to one story, Anglos stole his mining claim and killed his brother. In the Sierra Nevada, Murieta became one of the leaders of a band of outlaws known as "the Five Joaquíns." Between 1850 and 1853, they stole gold and horses and killed 19 people (mostly Chinese mine workers). They escaped three posses and killed three law officers. Poor Latinos in California often cheered when the outlaws attacked symbols of Anglo rule.

The governor of California created the California Rangers to capture the bandits. In 1853, a group of rangers had a fight with some Mexican men and killed two of them. The rangers claimed that one of the dead men was Murieta. They took the man's head as evidence of his death and preserved it in a jar of brandy. The head was exhibited throughout California, where spectators could pay one dollar to see it. However, some believed that the head was not Murieta's. Many people claimed to have seen him alive for years after 1853. (The head disappeared in the San Francisco earthquake of 1906.)

Murieta became the subject of legend. Many stories and songs portrayed him as a fierce fighter defending Mexicans against injustice. Stories about Murieta partly inspired the creation of the fictional character Zorro. For some Latinos, Murieta's name continues to stand for resistance against Anglo domination of Latinos in California. Yet the historical Murieta remains a mystery.

Strangers in Their Own Land

Illegal squatters, endless legal battles, and anti-Mexican prejudice all contributed to the decline of the Californios after the gold rush. Some of the great family names can still be found throughout California, but the Californios' ranching empire disappeared.

By the 1880s, Mexican Americans owned very little land in California. The loss of land reduced Latinos' standard of living and weakened their political power. Most Mexican Americans in California had little choice but to accept low-paying jobs at farms, ranches, mines, and railroads. Others moved to cities, where their agricultural skills were of little use. Anglo prejudice and low levels of education limited their ability to get better-paying professional jobs. Within the space of a lifetime, Californio culture had risen, peaked, and disappeared.

Conflict in the Borderlands

4

After 1848, the United States slowly took control of Mexico's old northern provinces. Mexican Americans struggled to hold on to their property, way of life, and place in society in the borderlands of Texas, New Mexico, and Arizona.

Cultural conflicts often developed between the Mexican Americans and Anglo Americans. Many of the Mexicans had been living in the region for generations and resented the Anglos as invaders who were overly ambitious, crude, and greedy. On the other hand, Anglos often considered themselves better than Mexican Americans. Anglos failed to understand the importance of leisure and strong family ties to Latinos. They considered Mexicans lazy and lacking in ambition. Many whites referred to Mexican Americans by the insulting term *greasers* (for their dark, slick hair).

The Mexicans were now shocked to find themselves the victims of U.S. racial policies. Segregated, or separate, restaurants, stores, and cemeteries for Mexicans became common in Texas and even in New Mexico and Arizona.

OPPOSITE During the 1850s, Mexican Americans were sometimes the victims of vigilante groups who took the law into their own hands. The vigilantes shot or hung suspected lawbreakers, sometimes simply because they spoke Spanish.

Most of the Anglo-American settlers were Protestants, while most Mexicans were Catholics. The Protestants did not have priests. Mexican Catholics could not understand how people could consider themselves Christian without priests. Anglo Protestants in the 1800s, however, thought that Catholicism was a strange, superstitious religion.

Even the traditional Catholic Church sometimes was prejudiced against Mexicans. Father Antonio José Martínez, a priest in Taos, created the first coeducational school in the territory and brought the first printing press to New Mexico. He also wanted to preserve the Mexican character of the Catholic Church in the territory. Martínez quarreled several times with Jean-Baptiste Lamy, the first bishop of New Mexico, over church law and tithes (taxes paid to the church). In 1855, Bishop Lamy implied that Mexican Catholics were not as smart or as moral as recent immigrants from the United States. These comments outraged many New Mexicans, and Martínez wrote articles for the *Santa Fe Gazette* criticizing Lamy and defending the culture of New Mexicans. In 1857, Martínez was excommunicated, or banned, by the Catholic Church.

Father Antonio José Martínez is shown in a photograph from the mid-1800s.

The Anglos Take Control

Important changes took place in southern Texas after 1850. Just as in California, Anglos used legal loopholes or brute force to take millions of acres of land from Mexican Americans. Anglos then combined these pieces of land into enormous ranches. By the 1890s, the McAllen/Young ranch measured 167,000 acres (68,000 ha), the Kennedy ranch stretched to 325,000 acres (132,000 ha), and the King ranch totaled an unbelievable 500,000 acres (202,000 ha). Many of the new Anglo land barons were not afraid to use violence to get their way. In 1878, the newspaper *Corpus Christi World* noted of one large rancher, "His neighbors mysteriously vanish whilst his territory extends over entire counties."

In 1850, Tejanos made up 32 percent of the workers in the state and owned 33 percent of the wealth. By 1870, Tejanos were 48 percent of the workforce but possessed only 11 percent of the wealth. In southern Texas, one-third of all ranches were in Anglo hands by 1900. Almost all the ranch hands were Mexican American. Only the smaller Tejano farmers managed to hold on to their land titles. Many Mexican Americans in Texas worked in the state's cotton industry, but Anglos owned all the best cotton land.

Anglos often used the law to discriminate against Latinos. Some towns banned Mexican fiestas. Anglo Texans and New Mexicans passed laws prohibiting traditional Mexican customs such as dancing the fandango, burying people under a church floor, holding religious festivities on Sunday, and marrying close relatives.

Many Tejanos left for Mexico, while very few Mexicans immigrated to Texas until the 1880s. The new state became much more Anglo in population, culture, and language. By the end of the 19th century, Mexican Americans in Texas had declined from an influential majority to a relatively powerless minority.

Anglo Violence

In many cases, Anglos used violence to keep Mexican Americans down. Spanish-language newspapers reported hundreds of lynchings of Mexicans, Chileans, and Peruvians in California and Texas.

Anglo-American mobs, with support from the Anglo communities, terrorized Mexican Americans throughout Texas. For example, the Corpus Christi reporter for the *Galveston Weekly News* wrote in 1855 that "the whole race of Mexicans here is becoming a useless commodity, being cheap, dog cheap. Eleven Mexicans, it is stated, have been found along the Nueces, in a *hung up* condition"—that is, lynched.

The state government regularly used a military organization known as the Texas Rangers to protect the large land and cattle operations of wealthy Anglos. The Texas Rangers were notorious for their brutality against Mexicans, killing hundreds, maybe thousands, of Mexican migrant workers without suffering any consequences. For example, in 1881, the Texas Rangers crossed the border into Mexico and illegally arrested Onofrio Baca, a Mexican migrant worker, on suspicion of murder. The Rangers promptly lynched him, leaving his body to hang for days in front of the courthouse.

In Arizona during the 1850s and 1860s, Anglo miners murdered Mexicans without any fear of punishment. In 1872, near the town of Blackwater, an Anglo mob burst into the home of Don Francisco Gándara Jr. and accused him of killing a white man. The mob murdered Gándara in front of his wife and daughters. It later turned out that Gándara was completely innocent.

Banditos: Heroes or Robbers?

In Texas, Anglos completely controlled the government. They kept their power by passing laws that prevented Mexican Americans from voting. Tejanos were allowed to elect leaders only in a few counties or towns where Mexicans remained a large majority of the population. Elsewhere, it was almost impossible for Mexicans to respond to Anglo attacks in a democratic way because they had no power in the legal system.

As a result, Mexican Americans sometimes used force to defend their rights. Some Mexicans became banditos, or bandits, as a way to survive. Others operated outside the law as a means of expressing complaints and frustrations with Anglo treatment. Banditos had a reputation for killing,

Juan Cortina

Juan Nepomuceno Cortina (1824–1894), was born in Mexico into a wealthy cattle-ranching family. Cortina particularly hated a group of Anglo lawyers and judges in southern Texas whom he accused of taking land from Mexican Texans.

In 1859, Cortina rode into Brownsville, Texas with about 50 men and seized control of the town. He issued a proclamation condemning the fact that so many people were "[prosecuted and robbed] for no other cause than that of being of Mexican origin."

Many Mexicans on both sides of the river idolized Cortina. His army soon grew to 500 men. Between 1859 and 1861, a small "Cortina War" took place along the 100-mile (160-km) stretch of the border from Brownsville to Rio Grande City. Under pressure from the U.S. government, Mexican authorities arrested him in 1875 and held him in prison in Mexico City until 1890.

robbing, rustling cattle, and destroying property. Anglos called them outlaws or desperados (from the Spanish for "desperate man"). Anglo settlers and upper-class Mexican Americans organized posses and even mobs known as vigilante groups to hunt for bandits. The vigilantes often shot and killed people simply because they spoke Spanish.

The Spanish-speaking poor, however, often honored the bandits as rebels and provided them shelter from the law. At one time or another, most Mexican-American bandits were compared to Robin Hood, the legendary English outlaw who stole from the rich and gave to the poor. The most famous were Juan Cortina and Gregorio Cortez in Texas and Joaquín Murieta, Juan Flores, and Tiburcio Vásquez in California.

The Gorras Blancas

Unlike California and Texas, New Mexico had been a center of colonists from Mexico from the earliest days of Spanish rule. At the end of the Mexican-American War, far more Mexicans lived in New Mexico than in California and Texas combined. Given the choice of Mexican or U.S. citizenship, most Spanish-speaking residents chose to remain in New Mexico, where Mexican Americans remained a majority of the population until the 20th century. They formed a community that managed to keep some political power. Miguel Otero and Donaciano Vigal were well-known Latino politicians in New Mexico before 1880.

However, Anglos slowly took control of the territory. The U.S. government appointed the territorial governor, and only one Latino served in this position from 1848 until New Mexico became a state in 1912. By 1900, Anglo settlers, land companies, and lawyers held 80 percent of former Mexican lands.

Resenting the powers that had taken their land, some Mexican Americans began organizing people to resist unjust Anglo laws. In the late 1880s, Mexicans created their own vigilante groups, such as the Gorras Blancas (White Caps) in San Miguel County. The Gorras Blancas cut down barbed-wire fences, destroyed railroad tracks and telegraph lines, and burned Anglo barns and ranches. Their goal was to gain back communal Mexican land that Anglo newcomers to the region, such as the Las Vegas Land Cattle Company, were fencing off as private property.

The Gorras Blancas asked New Mexicans not to work for anyone unless the organization approved the work and the salaries they would be receiving. Railroad workers were encouraged to strike for higher pay, and timber cutters who prepared railroad ties were urged to demand

Corridos

In the mid-1800s, a new type of song, known as the *corrido*, became popular in the southwestern United States. The corrido is a fast-paced folk ballad sung to polka, waltz, or march music. Popular corridos told the story of gun battles, wars, crimes, love affairs, cattle drives, the coming of the railroad, and the lives of bandits. The authors of most of these ballads are unknown.

If a corrido was popular, printing shops in cities on both sides of the border would publish it. Corridos were meant to be entertaining. In the late 1800s, they also served as news reports and history textbooks for illiterate Mexicans.

higher prices from the railroad. In March 1890, the Gorras Blancas put up posters all over the town of Las Vegas, New Mexico, stating that their purpose was "to protect the rights and interests of the people in general and especially those of the helpless classes. . . ." The Gorras Blancas slowly died out as an organized movement by 1892, but the issue of land grants continued to affect New Mexico society well into the next century.

Range Wars in New Mexico

Many Latinos in New Mexico kept herds of sheep. In the early and mid-1800s, they grazed these sheep on open, unfenced public lands. Sheep could survive droughts better than cattle, and sheep prices were more stable. One man and two trained dogs could handle 800 sheep.

When Anglo cattle ranchers arrived in New Mexico in the 1870s, they fought the sheepherders in range wars. The cattle ranchers seized farmland and open grasslands and put up barbed-wire fences. Sheepherders cut the wire and attacked the cattle. The fighting between cattle ranchers and sheepherders continued for the next 30 years. The most famous and violent incidents occurred between Latinos and two competing groups of Anglos in Lincoln County, New Mexico, in the 1870s. By 1900, the cattle ranchers and sheepherders had come to an uneasy truce. At that time, New Mexico was producing almost 20 million pounds (9million kg) of wool from 4 million sheep and shipping about 300,000 cattle out of state every year. Latino workers played a key role in both industries in New Mexico.

Working within the System

Mexican Americans did not always answer violence with violence. They also tried to work within the system by forming labor unions and electing sympathetic politicians.

In 1883, Juan Gómez led several hundred cowboys on a strike against ranch owners in Texas. This was the first time Latinos participated in an organized labor activity in the United States. Many Latino workers joined the Knights of Labor, the largest labor union in the United States in the 1880s. Mexican-American miners in New Mexico, Arizona, and Colorado all experimented with forming Latino unions during the 1880s and 1890s.

In 1888, Juan José Herrera founded the Caballeros de Labor in New Mexico. This was one of the first Latino labor unions in the Southwest. In 1890, Herrera founded El Partido del Pueblo Unido (The United People's Party), the first Latino political party in U.S. history. The party worked with the Anglo Populist Party to fight against political corruption in New Mexico.

In 1890, Félix Martínez, a New Mexico businessman, took over the leadership of El Partido del Pueblo Unido. Two years later, New Mexicans elected him to the territorial council. By the time of his death in 1916, Martínez was probably the most famous Latino in the United States.

Latinos in the borderlands faced many challenges in the late 1800s: Anglo prejudice, the theft of their land, and the struggle for political power. Latinos used a variety of methods, both legal and illegal, to deal with their situation as a minority group in an Anglo-controlled world.

Mexican-American Life

5

In 1876, Porfirio Díaz took power in Mexico and began his 35-year rule. Díaz tried to modernize Mexico, but his policies broke up the collective lands that Mexican villagers depended on to survive. On collective farms, the whole village instead of an individual owned the land and all the villagers farmed it together. Millions of Mexican farmers were forced into a life of unemployment or seasonal work. In general, living standards collapsed all across Mexico.

Meanwhile, in the United States, businesses were searching the world for natural resources, cheap labor, and new places to sell their products. Díaz encouraged U.S. investment and trade. He actually sold three-quarters of the nation's mineral wealth to foreign interests. Between 1860 and 1890, U.S. trade with Mexico increased from $7 million to $64 million. Mexico became a land of peace even though half the rural population lived almost like slaves. By 1900, about nine of every ten Mexicans were landless day laborers.

OPPOSITE Two Mexican vendors, dressed in traditional clothing, carry their wares on their backs in this photograph from the late 1800s.

Mexican-American Population Increase

During Díaz's reign, about 15,000 miles (24,000 km) of railroads were built in Mexico. The railroad made it easier for people to move from the heavily settled area around Mexico City to the less-developed northern regions of Mexico. However, this freedom of movement also encouraged immigration to the United States. The Mexican-American population of the United States increased from about 100,000 in 1850 to about 275,000 in 1880.

In the 1880s and 1890s, most Mexican immigrants were looking for seasonal work. A few were escaping political persecution in Mexico. Ranch hands entered southern California from Chihuahua, Sonora, Durango, and other western states in Mexico. Many of these immigrants scattered into Arizona, Colorado, Nevada, and even the Pacific Northwest in search of jobs or new mining opportunities. By 1900, an estimated 500,000 Mexican Americans lived in the United States.

Vaqueros and Cowboys

Mexicans were experts in ranching long before Anglos arrived. As early as the 1600s, Spanish settlers raised cattle north of the Rio Grande and drove them to market in Mexico City. The drivers of the cattle were called vaqueros. They were rough, hard-working mestizos skilled in riding horses and handling cattle. The practice of rounding up and roping cows on horseback began with Mexican vaqueros.

In the 1830s, when Anglo settlers arrived in Texas, millions of wild longhorn cattle roamed the brush country. The people who could round up the cattle and drive them to market could make huge profits. By the 1870s, Texas cowboys and vaqueros were driving herds of thousands of longhorn cattle over established trails to the Kansas "cow towns." From there, railroads carried them to the hungry cities in the East and the Midwest.

At the peak of the open range in the 1870s, about one out of every three cowboys in the western United States was a Mexican vaquero. Anglo cowboys learned many of their techniques from vaqueros. Several symbols associated with Texas cowboys were orig-inally Mexican. The high-heeled boots of the vaquros

These vaqueros are branding longhorn cattle in this woodcut from the mid-1800s.

supported their feet in the stirrups of their saddles. Their wide-brimmed hats (sombreros) shielded their faces from the sun. To protect themselves from cactus, sagebrush, and other desert plants that could scratch or cut them, vaque-ros wore leather trousers known as *chaparreras*—chaps in English.

The vaqueros' vocabulary also became part of the language of the United States. The English word *buckaroo* comes from the Mexican *vaquero*. The word *rancho* turned into *ranch,* and the vaquero's *la riata* became *lariat* in English.

After the 1870s, the cattle-driving industry began to decline. A series of droughts and hard winters forced many outfits out of business. More railroads meant less need to drive cattle long distances. The invention of barbed wire in 1873 doomed the open range.

When the open-range era ended, Mexican Americans worked as seasonal employees at ranches. This was a different way of life. Ranch owners in the new West no longer paid their workers in the off-season or allowed them to stay on the ranch for free. Ranch hands, both Anglo and Latino, now had to travel around to make enough money to survive and feed their families.

Many Latinos worked in the Nevada silver mines, like the miners shown here changing shift in the 1870s.

Mexican Miners

In mining, as in ranching, Mexicans often had more knowledge and experience than Anglo newcomers to the western United States. Mexicans taught Anglos how to use a *batea* (a flat-bottomed pan) to remove gold from streams and rivers. They also taught the Anglos how to crush gold-bearing rocks with a tool called an *arrastra* and how to use mercury to refine gold.

Mexican Americans had discovered many of the silver, gold, and mineral resources of the western United States. For example, Mexicans discovered the famous New

Almaden quicksilver mine near San Jose, California. However, digging deep mine shafts required a great deal of money and many low-paid miners. Landless Mexicans and Mexican Americans filled the need for cheap labor. One visitor to the mines wrote that "the laborers are all Mexicans and have generally served a sort of apprenticeship in the silver mines of Spanish America. . . . [The laborers] are fair specimens of the reckless, improvident [irresponsible] Spanish-American race. . . . It is of little consequence how much or how little they receive."

In the 1870s, one of the world's richest copper deposits was discovered in southern Arizona and a corner of New Mexico. Not surprisingly, Arizona's immigrant population increased from 4,348 in 1870 to 9,330 in 1880. Most of this increase was because of the arrival of Mexican miners.

By the 1880s, mining had become an expensive industry. Large corporations ran mines because they had enough money to dig the deep mine shafts. Miners, like vaqueros, were slowly becoming company employees who worked for set wages.

Commercial Agriculture

By the 1890s, advances in science and technology led to changes in farming in the western United States. Farmers learned to build reservoirs to hold water and to irrigate their fields carefully. In some places, they could farm year-round. Ambitious men purchased old ranch lands throughout the southwestern United States and turned them into farms. They grew crops such as grains, fruit, and an assortment of

Mexican-American Railroad Workers

In the late 1800s, there was a railroad-building boom across the United States. Mexican Americans built large stretches of these railroads. After the U.S. Congress limited Chinese immigration in 1882, railroads like the Southern Pacific and the Santa Fe hired Mexican Americans to build the new lines across the desert. By 1900, more than half of the track-laying crews and service crews on southwestern railroads were Latino. The railroads made it possible to ship products from Texas, Arizona, and California to cities in the East and other world markets.

vegetables. Large farms were needed in order to make a decent profit. However, large farms required a lot of workers. In order to fill this demand, Anglo farmers recruited Mexican workers to pick, process, pack, and ship their crops.

Many Mexican farm workers were hired by contractors who supervised and paid them. The contractor system often worked badly for Mexicans. Some labor contractors provided very poor living conditions or refused to pay their workers in order to increase their own profit. Yet Mexico's economy under Porfirio Díaz was so poor that Mexican farm workers in the United States would not risk the loss of their jobs by complaining. They thus got a reputation of being passive, hardworking, and cheap.

La Alianza Hispano-Americana

In order to survive and prosper in the United States, new immigrants often rely on people of their own nationality for support. Mexican Americans began to create mutual-aid societies (*mutualistas*) in the United States in the 1890s. Mutualistas allowed members to combine their resources to offer loans, life insurance, temporary housing, and employment assistance. Mutualistas also sponsored dances, lectures, and other social events.

The most important mutualista in the Southwest was *La Alianza Hispano-Americana,* or the Hispanic-American Alliance. This organization was founded in Tucson, Arizona, in 1894 by newspaper editor Carlos Velasco. La Alianza Hispano-Americana quickly gained membership and spread throughout the southwestern United States. The mutualista became a force to protect the civil rights and workers' rights of Mexican Americans. By 1930, La Alianza Hispano-Americana counted more than 17,000 members, some as far north as Chicago.

Almost everywhere Latinos lived, they formed organizations for mutual aid. In the 1890s, Los Angeles was still a small city with fewer than 50,000 people. Yet it featured Latino clubs that provided lectures and musical performances. In 1897, a group of Los Angeles Catholic women established *El Hogar Feliz,* "the Happy Home," to serve the Mexican community. The house, located in the middle of a Mexican-American neighborhood, included a medical clinic and a school.

Mexican-American Women in the United States

Before 1848, married women on the Mexican frontier could own and keep property in their own family name after marriage. When they married, Spanish law assumed they owned a one-half interest in the property they shared with their husbands. This was not the case for Anglo women. Before 1848, most married women in the United States could not own any property in their own names. The property all belonged to their husbands.

When the United States conquered the northern half of Mexico in 1848, Latino women lost their legal advantages. Mexican women who remained in the region became subject to U.S. law. However, many Latino single women or widows owned property or managed and worked their own land with the help of children or hired hands.

The California gold rush drew some Latino women to the mining camps. Women went to seek their fortune as cooks, laundresses, and gambling house operators. When the mining boom ended, many of these women traveled through the region in search of work. Others returned to Mexico.

This photograph of a school class from the 1890s shows a number of Latino children among those attending the North Public School in Las Vegas, Nevada.

Changes in Mexican-American Family Life

As the economy of the southwestern United States changed, the roles of men and women changed. When Mexican Americans lost their land, family life became less secure. Mexican men found themselves traveling around the southwestern United States to find work on farms, on ranches, or in mines. Some women, too, left their homes in search of work.

Much of this work was only temporary. In addition, many of the new jobs in mining and railroad construction were very dangerous. Work accidents left increasing numbers of Mexican widows and orphans. Mutualistas provided benefits to women if their husbands died. However, the number of female-headed households slowly began to rise.

The new economy pushed women into working for money wages. They labored in the fields or in restaurants, hotels, packinghouses, and laundries. In cities and on farms, Latino family members pooled their money to survive. Some women worked at home by taking in laundry, housing boarders, or quilting, ironing, or sewing for pay.

In some ways, Latinos—both men and women—were very conservative about equal rights for women. Most Latinos believed that families could function only if women always followed what men said. Some Latinos in New Mexico even protested the creation of public schools that educated boys and girls together. Latinos divorced at a much lower rate than Anglos.

Only a small percentage of Mexican Americans supported the women's suffrage movement. (Suffrage is the

Antonio Coronel

Not all Mexican-American lives were unstable in the 1800s. Antonio Coronel (1817–1894) was a rancher, educator, art collector, and politician. He came to southern California with his father at the age of 17. Coronel become mayor of Los Angeles in 1853, Los Angeles city council member in 1854, and state treasurer in 1866. As mayor, he established Los Angeles's first department of public works. He worked hard to defend Latino land titles.

Coronel had a large art collection, which he donated to the Los Angeles Chamber of Commerce. He supported efforts to build a library and organized festivals celebrating Mexican traditions. In 1883, Coronel helped found the Historical Society of Southern California. He also edited *Ramona,* a romantic novel of southern California history by New England novelist Helen Hunt Jackson. *Ramona* was published in 1884 and became a huge best seller.

right to vote.) In 1877, one Latino priest stated in the newspaper *La revista católica* that women's suffrage would destroy the family. However, when women did receive the right to vote in Colorado in 1893, some Latino women ran for office and held some local positions.

The Creation of Barrios

The majority of Mexicans who settled in the United States after 1880 clustered in barrios. A barrio was a neighborhood where Mexican Americans lived. A barrio might be just a few shacks in a dusty New Mexico town or as large as eastern Los Angeles. One Mexican described the barrio in Sacramento at the turn of the century as "a neighborhood of leftover houses. The cheapest rents were in the back quarters of the rooming houses, the basements, and the rundown rentals in the alleys." With the decline of the rancho tradition of year-round support for ranch hands, many Mexican Americans lived in a city for at least part of the year.

Barrios existed through a combination of Anglo force and Latino choice. Anglos did not want to live with Mexicans and often refused to sell houses to Mexican buyers. Some Latinos who dared to move into an Anglo neighborhood were physically attacked. This lack of welcome forced Mexican Americans to settle in areas where other Mexican Americans lived. These areas were sometimes rundown or dangerous. Local governments, usually controlled by Anglos, often spent no money on barrios. They were the last sections of town to receive proper water systems, sewer systems, and electricity.

On the other hand, most Mexican Americans and new Mexican immigrants probably preferred living among people who knew their native language and culture. The Catholic Church was often the center of social and religious life. In the barrio, there might be bullfights, rodeos, horse races, and fiestas, including the celebration of Mexican Independence Day (September 16) and Cinco de Mayo (May 5). Cinco de Mayo is a Mexican holiday that celebrates the victory of Mexican soldiers over French invaders at Puebla, Mexico, on May 5, 1862.

In the barrio, large extended families and community life flourished. In 1991, at age 84, one woman recalled the history of her family in New Mexico: "Social life at San Miguel in the 1860s up to the early 1900s as I remember hearing about it, centered around my great-grandmother Iñez's big living room. Whenever the people in the area had any kind of a meeting, a dance, baptism, or special occasion, they used that room." Their extended families and the barrio were the center of life for most Mexican Americans.

Preserving the
Spanish Language

Like most immigrants, Mexican Americans were not sure whether to hold on to their traditional language, give it up for English, or become bilingual. Mexican Americans who valued their past and wanted to preserve their identity usually tried to speak Spanish and teach it to their children. They were most successful in areas where Latinos still had some political or economic power. Spanish also was spoken freely in the barrios, where segregation kept the English language away. Elizabeth Post, a schoolteacher in Ehrenberg, Arizona, wrote in 1872, "I had fifteen pupils not one of whom knew any English, and I knew nothing of Spanish."

In the 1870s, the legislature of the New Mexico Territory still operated mostly in Spanish and only two of fourteen counties had switched to jury trials in English. Most of New Mexico's public schools conducted instruction entirely in Spanish or bilingually.

Eventually, however, Mexican Americans who did not know English found themselves at a disadvantage in the courts and schools and while looking for work. The question of which language to speak and teach to children would continue to be an issue in the Latino community into the 21st century.

Fast Fact

In the Colorado Territory, a law passed in 1867 established bilingual education in every school with at least 25 non-English-speaking children. The Colorado state constitution of 1875, drafted in both English and Spanish, specifically protected the rights of Spanish-speaking citizens and required that all laws had to be printed in both languages.

The New Economic Order

By 1900, the southwestern United States was a very different place from half a century before. Large corporations, powerful railroads, and huge commercial farms led the new economic system. This economy created many jobs for unskilled laborers willing to work for low wages in difficult conditions. Landless Latinos often filled this role. However, some Mexican Americans, such as those in northern New Mexico and southern Texas, continued to live in the countryside as their ancestors had for the last century.

No single picture can describe all the Mexican Americans in the United States in the late 1800s. Some were rich and some were poor. Some spoke only Spanish and others could not learn English fast enough. Some welcomed U.S. citizenship, like Miguel Otero, the New Mexico territorial governor from 1897 to 1906 (and son of an earlier New Mexico politician of the same name). Others resented the presence of the United States in what used to be northern Mexico.

However, one constant feature of Latino life in the southwestern United States was Anglo prejudice. As a U.S. mechanic noted around 1900, "They will never pay a Mexican what he's really worth compared with a white man. I know a Mexican that's the best blacksmith I ever knew. . . . But they pay him $1.50 a day as a helper, working under an American blacksmith who gets 7 dollars a day."

The Spanish Caribbean

6

Mexicans were not the only Latinos to play an important role in the United States in the 19th century. Many Spanish-speaking people from the Caribbean, especially Cuba, also made an impact. After the Spanish lost their empire in South America, some Cubans hoped for political change in Cuba. However, they were not united as to what course to take.

Independentistas wanted to rebel against Spain to create an independent republic of Cuba. They pointed to the success of Simón Bolívar's revolts against Spain in South America. However, most wealthy Cubans in the early 1800s considered this position too radical. They feared that an independent Cuba would lead to the end of slavery and possibly a race war on the island.

Reformistas wanted to reform the relationship between Spain and Cuba. They admired Spain and Spanish culture and wished to remain a province under the Spanish crown and Spanish protection. Reformistas thought that a war for independence would be long and bloody and serve no

OPPOSITE Ships full of gold-seekers left the eastern United States bound for California and landed in Panama, as shown in this woodcut from the 1800s. The passengers then crossed the isthmus by land and reboarded ships bound for San Francisco.

purpose in the end. Instead, their main goal was for Spain to allow native-born Cubans to take part in the government of Cuba.

Anexionistas wanted Cuba to join the United States as a state. They pointed to the example of Florida, annexed to the United States in 1821. By becoming part of the United States, Cubans would exchange the rule of a declining colonial power for that of a rising world power. Some anexionistas admired the U.S. political system. Most, however, wanted to preserve slavery, as did the U.S. South, which was one of the world's largest slave societies in the early 1800s.

The Cuban Community
in the United States

In the early 1800s, U.S. ships importing sugar and molasses from Cuba sometimes carried Cuban immigrants as well. Many of them settled in port cities in the United States. As early as 1825, there was a small Cuban presence in the northeastern United States. This was 20 years before the Mexican-American War added a huge Latino population to the United States.

Many of these Cubans lived in New York City. Several waterfront boardinghouses specialized in sheltering Latino Caribbean immigrants. Cuban immigrants in New York City, numbering more than 500 in 1845, worked on merchant vessels, on the docks, and in local factories. The Cuban-Puerto Rican Benevolent Merchants' Association, founded in 1830, reflected the growth of trade connections between the Spanish Caribbean and the United States.

In the decades before the Civil War, Cuban merchants and workers were joined by Cubans who were fleeing Spanish rule. A group of famous Cuban families, such as the Quesadas, the Arangos, and the Mantillas, made their home in New York City. The family of José de Rivera, a wealthy sugar and wine trader, lived in an elegant house in Bridgeport, Connecticut.

Cubans in the United States were not united on their approach to Spanish rule in Cuba. Gaspar Betancourt Cisneros, who decided to stay in the United States after attending college in Philadelphia, Pennsylvania, was a noted antislavery anexionista. He was unusual because most anexionistas were proslavery. José Antonio Saco, a writer who lived in the United States from 1824 to 1832, was a major reformista. José María Heredia, a noted Cuban poet and writer, was one of the chief independentistas.

Latino Literature in the United States

Many of the Cuban immigrants to the northeastern United States were well educated. These Cuban writers created the earliest examples of Latino-American literature. In 1825, José María Heredia published the first collection of poems by a Latino writer in the United States. Heredia, who lived in the United States from 1823 to 1836, remains a famous poet of Spanish America. He wrote most of his poems in the United States, including his most famous poem, "Ode to Niagara," about his visit to Niagara Falls.

In 1858, a group of Cuban poets in New York published a collection of Latino poetry called *El laúd del desterrado (The*

José María de Heredia, from a photograph taken in the late 1800s.

Lute of the Exiled). The book gathered together the writings of Cuban poets who lived in exile in the United States and supported Cuba's independence from Spain.

Another noted Cuban writer was Cirillo Villaverde, who came to the United States in 1849. While living in New York, he wrote *Cecilia Valdés,* one of the most famous novels about 19th-century Cuba. It explores the problems of slavery, racism, and Spanish rule in Cuba.

Throughout the 1800s, Cubans organized many Spanish-language newspapers in the United States. *El Habanero* was one of the first. It was published by Félix Varela in Philadelphia and then in New York City from 1824 to 1826. In *El Habanero,* Varela appealed for Cuban independence and supported human rights, religious freedom, and cooperation between the English- and Spanish-speaking communities. In 1828, Varela began writing for *El Mensajero Semanal,* another Cuban New York newspaper founded by José Antonio Saco.

Cubans in New Orleans

Before the Civil War, New Orleans, Louisiana, was the second-leading port of entry for immigrants to the United States. Between 1820 and 1860, more than 550,000 immigrants came through New Orleans. It was also one of the few U.S. cities in the 19th century to draw immigrants from

Spain and Latin America. The city was popular with Latinos because it was so close to Latin America and maintained regular shipping service to Cuba and Central America.

Cubans in New Orleans were divided between independentistas and anexionistas. Both sides produced their own short-lived Spanish-language newspapers. Many Cubans in New Orleans were friends with wealthy Southern slaveholders. In the U.S. Civil War, hundreds of Cuban residents in Florida and Louisiana would give the Confederate rebels sympathy and military support.

Cubans influenced New Orleans in more than just politics. Louis Morceau Gottschalk was a famous New Orleans piano player and composer who visited Cuba several times. In the 1850s, he began introducing Cuban elements into songs like *"Ojos Criollos"* and *"Escenas Campestres Cubanas."* By the end of the century, Mexican and Cuban musicians were playing important roles in New Orleans's famous ragtime movement. Latino rhythms were later absorbed into African-

Félix Varela

Félix Varela (1788–1853), was a Cuban patriot, novelist, journalist, philosopher, and Catholic priest. He came to the United States in 1823 and became one of the leading Catholic figures in New York City. In 1826, Varela published *Jicotencal,* one of the first historical novels ever written in the United States. In another book, *Cartas a Elpido,* Varela argued that the Catholic religion was not against human reason. Varela was also a leader of the Cuban independence movement.

Varela was a social reformer. In 1832, a cholera epidemic spread through the slums of New York. Varela tended the sick and created orphanages. He also organized some of the first children's day care centers in the United States. Varela became the defender and protector of New York's extremely poor Irish immigrant community. In 1997, the U.S. Post Office issued a stamp to honor him.

American styles in jazz. In that way, the New Orleans Latino community was a musical melting pot.

A Canal in Central America?

Until 1849, people in the United States barely thought about Central America. Then gold was discovered in California. Rather than going overland across the United States or sailing around the southern tip of South America, thousands of U.S. migrants to the West found it faster, cheaper, and safer to sail to Panama, cross the 48 miles (77 km) of land, and sail up the Pacific coast to California. In the United States, a railroad across the country would not be completed until 1869. In Panama, however, a U.S. company completed the Panama Railroad connecting the two oceans across the isthmus in 1855.

The Panama Railroad took five years to build and cost the lives of 9,000 workers, who died from disease, poor sanitary conditions, and overwork. Yet between 1855 and 1869, the railroad carried 600,000 people and $750 million in gold from California to the eastern United States. A scattering of Panamanian immigrants now began appearing in New York and San Francisco.

The development of California after the gold rush created a need for improved communication between the distant coasts of the United States. A canal across Central America, connecting the Atlantic and Pacific Oceans, seemed to be the answer. A canal would save the long trip around Cape Horn and cut weeks of sailing time between New York and San Francisco.

Two main routes for a canal were possible. One cut directly through the Isthmus of Panama and the other was a river-lake-canal route across Nicaragua. The United States did not own land in either of these places. Yet because of its desire to build the canal, the United States became deeply involved in Central American affairs. The U.S. government began writing treaties concerning Central America. In addition, private U.S. citizens, called filibusters, began invading Caribbean islands and Central American nations.

This map shows the route of the Old Panama Railroad from the town of Colon on the Caribbean Sea to Panama City on the Pacific coast.

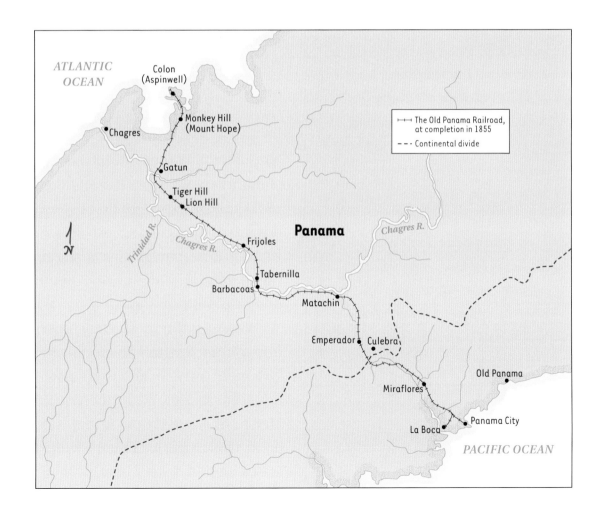

William Walker and Nicaragua

The most famous filibuster of all was doctor, lawyer, and journalist William Walker. Walker found adventure by invading Nicaragua. The nation was important to U.S. foreign policy because it was one of the two possibilities for a canal between the Atlantic and Pacific Oceans.

In 1855, Walker landed in Nicaragua with 60 men. Amazingly, he managed to capture Granada and declare himself the dictator of Nicaragua. In 1857, local Nicaraguans drove Walker from power.

To many white Southerners Walker was a hero. Ten thousand admirers came out to greet him when he returned to New Orleans. Walker made two more unsuccessful attempts to conquer Nicaragua. In 1860, Walker was captured by the British. He was delivered to the government of Honduras, which had him executed by firing squad.

Filibustering

Before the Civil War, many white Southerners looked toward Cuba as a slaveholding area that could be annexed to the United States as a slave state. In 1848, President James Polk offered to buy Cuba from Spain for $100 million. In response, the Spanish minister declared, "Sooner than see the island transferred to any power, they would prefer seeing it sunk in the ocean."

Since Spain would not give up Cuba peacefully, some private filibusters (from the Spanish *filibustero*, describing someone who defied authority) took the matter into their own hands. From 1830 to 1860, dozens of filibustering expeditions left U.S. soil, aimed at conquering Cuba, Mexico, Central and South America, and even Canada.

White Southerners were upset because the Spanish would not sell Cuba and private filibusters could not seem to steal it. In the Ostend Manifesto of 1854, proslavery U.S. politicians suggested that the United States should take Cuba by force.

The refusal of the Northern states to agree with this position angered many white Southerners. Edmund Ruffin, a proslavery scientist, declared that "the conquest of [Cuba] by any civilized power, would be a benefit to the conquered and to the world . . . the people are worthless, and afford no hope of their improvement . . . and their extinction will be a benefit to America."

Filibustering to Cuba peaked between 1848 and 1856 and declined after the U.S. Civil War. Some Cubans in the United States viewed the filibusters as heroes who dared to fight against the Spanish. Others saw them as conquerors who simply wanted to extend slavery.

Narciso López and Cuba

The Venezuelan-born filibuster Narciso López tried three separate times to invade Cuba with money from Southern slave owners. In his second attempt in 1850, he actually seized Cardenas, a small port 8 miles (13 km) east of Havana. The invaders, failed in their attempt to begin a revolution against Spain.

In 1851, López decided to launch another invasion of Cuba. This time, the filibusters landed at Playtas. However, Spanish troops defeated the invaders. In a trial, López's men admitted that they were invaders. Some, including López, were executed in Havana's public square.

Between 1848 and 1860, Cuban exiles, U.S. citizens, and the U.S. government had taken a strong interest in Cuba. For all that, the island seemed no closer to independence from Spain.

Cuba Libre

7

By the 1860s, Spanish taxes were very high in the colony of Cuba. Spanish trade restrictions raised prices and prevented Cuba from developing any crop but sugarcane. Almost no native Cubans held governmental positions on the island. Many criollos (people born in Latin America to Spanish parents) and middle-class islanders concluded that political independence rather than reform could best solve their problems.

Cuban unhappiness finally boiled over in 1868. On October 10, Carlos Manuel de Céspedes, a criollo plantation owner, began a revolt. Joined by 37 other planters, Céspedes freed his slaves and formed them into a rebel army. He appealed to Cubans to take up arms and throw out the greedy colonial government. Céspedes's call is known as *El Grito de Yara* ("the Cry of Yara") after the small town where the uprising broke out. It began a movement for Cuban independence from Spain known as the Ten Years' War (1868–1878).

There were no major battles between Cuban rebels and the Spanish army in this war. Instead, the fighting consisted of guerrilla warfare, especially in the eastern part of the island known as Oriente. About 50,000 Cubans and

OPPOSITE This photograph of Carlos Manuel de Céspedes and his wife was taken shortly after Céspedes was sworn in as the provisional president of Cuba in 1933. Céspedes's father (who had the same name) is considered by many to be the father of Cuban nation.

more than 200,000 Spanish perished in the Ten Years' War. Yet when the war finally ended in a draw, almost nothing had changed.

Some Cuban leaders in the Ten Years' War had received their military experience in the United States. For example, Federico Fernández Cavada served as an officer in the Union Army until he was captured at the famous Battle of Gettysburg in 1863. Cavada was held as a prisoner of war at Libby Prison in Virginia until January 1864. After the war, he published *Libby Life,* a memoir of his prison experience. When the Ten Years' War began, Cavada volunteered to join the Cuban army and became chief of staff. In 1871, the Spanish captured him. U.S. president Ulysses S. Grant and other U.S. generals asked for mercy, but the Spanish executed him.

The United States Tries to Annex the Dominican Republic

Santo Domingo, now known as the Dominican Republic, was a former Spanish colony that shared the island of Hispaniola with the nation of Haiti. By the 1860s, many U.S. investors owned very profitable land, forests, and mines in the country. However, Santo Domingo did not have a stable government in the 1800s. Dictators often ruled the country.

One leader of the Dominican Republic, Buenaventura Baez, gained and lost the presidency of the country six times between 1849 and 1878. During some of his years out of power, he lived in New York City. In 1869, Baez was back in power. Amazingly, he offered to hand over his bankrupt nation to the United States for less than $2 million.

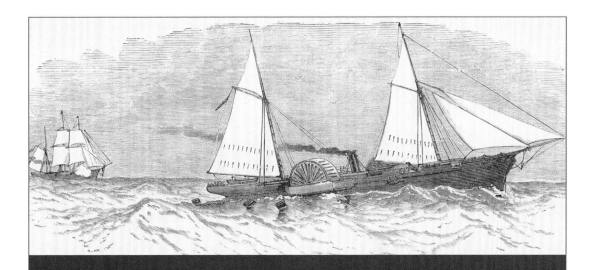

The *Virginius* Incident of 1873

During the Ten Years' War, Cuban exiles in the United States held mass meetings, produced propaganda, and organized expeditions to help the rebels. Some North Americans also wanted to help the Cubans, whom they considered freedom fighters.

The *Virginius* was a Cuban-owned vessel that had been illegally flying the U.S. flag for years while it smuggled weapons and supplies from the United States to Cuban rebels. In 1873, a Spanish warship captured the *Virginius*. After secret courts-martial in Santiago, Cuba, the Spanish executed Captain Joseph Fry and 52 crew members and passengers. Some of those executed were citizens of Great Britain and the United States.

This insult to the U.S. flag caused outbursts against Spain from Boston to New Orleans. The U.S. government demanded an apology and a large payment of damages. War between the United States and Spain seemed very close. However, the two countries eventually reached a settlement. Many Cubans and Cuban Americans considered Captain Fry a hero and a martyr for the cause of Cuban independence.

Many people in the United States supported annexation of Santo Domingo, including investors, naval leaders, and President Grant. However, public opinion was generally against this plan. Many whites did not want to annex lands filled with dark-skinned people. Influential editor E. L. Godkin condemned the idea that "ignorant Catholic Spanish Negroes" could become U.S. citizens. Despite President Grant's support, the Senate defeated the treaty to annex Santo Domingo in 1870.

A Canal in Panama

In 1865, Ferdinand de Lesseps became world famous by completing the 100-mile (160-km) Suez Canal. This tremendous project connected the Mediterranean Sea and the Red Sea. In 1879, a French company headed by the now 74-year-old de Lesseps announced that he would build a sea-level canal connecting the Atlantic and the Pacific across Panama.

The U.S. government was stunned. People in the United States were shocked that someone would actually try to build the Central American canal, and a European company at that. In 1880, U.S. president Rutherford Hayes declared that any proposed canal would be "virtually a part of the coast line of the United States" and that "the policy of this country is a canal under American control . . . either an American canal or no canal must be our motto."

De Lesseps's company began the project, but disease and construction problems forced the company into bankruptcy before it came close to finishing the canal, However, the United States once again became very interested in building a Central American canal. The U.S. government knew that this would require strong U.S. involvement in Central America and the Caribbean, especially Cuba, to ensure the successful defense of any canal, as well as other American investments in the area. The United States would eventually complete the Panama Canal in 1914, but not before American armies, power, and money had completely changed the Caribbean and Central America.

Building the Panama Canal was dangerous work. Here, a premature explosion threatens the crew and damages valuable equipment.

José Martí in New York

In 1880, José Martí, a Cuban poet and journalist, arrived in New York. Martí had been exiled from Cuba for trying to start a revolution against Spain for Cuban independence. For the next 15 years, Martí, the leading figure in the Cuban independence movement, rallied Cubans in the United States to free Cuba from Spanish control.

Martí was a prolific writer. He wrote volumes of poetry and prose. He translated novels and poetry from Spanish to English and from English to Spanish. He published a magazine for children. His writing was so admired that the governments of Uruguay, Paraguay, and Argentina appointed him their consul, or representative, in New York.

Martí's main source of income in New York, however, was journalism. He wrote hundreds of articles and essays for North American and Latin American newspapers. He covered the news of the day, the lives of leading citizens and the activities of high society, holidays, elections, labor struggles, murders, trials, and prizefights. His articles were reprinted in newspapers all over Latin America, making him one of the world's first international journalists. Martí became good friends with Charles Anderson Dana, the wealthy, powerful publisher of the *New York Sun*. Dana was a strong supporter of Cuban independence. He gave Martí a way to make a living and a platform from which to argue for Cuban independence.

One of Martí's constant worries was that people in the Spanish Caribbean and South America did not really understand the United States. In 1883, Martí became chief editor of *La América,* a magazine with offices in New York City. Martí said he wanted "to explain the mind of the United States of the North to the minds of those who are in spirit and will someday be in form, the United States of South America." He later wrote in the magazine, "Our greatest desire is to bring together the souls and the hands of our Latin American peoples."

The longer Martí lived in New York, the more he worried that the United States was trying to control the Caribbean and South America. He warned his readers repeatedly that North American control of the Caribbean would be a disaster for Cuba. Martí criticized the United States as it began taking over other countries, such as the Pacific islands of Samoa in 1889 and Hawaii in 1890. Martí feared that the United States might have similar designs on Puerto Rico and Cuba.

Florida's Cuban Community in Key West

In 1831, 50 Cuban tobacco workers opened a cigar factory in Key West, Florida. However, a Cuban community did not really develop there

La Lectura

Latino cigar workers were noted for their practice of reading aloud in the factories. This was known as *la lectura*. A reader on a platform on the factory floor would read books or newspapers out loud so the workers who stemmed the tobacco leaves and rolled the cigars could hear. Sometimes, the reader would repeat a certain part of a particular book several times so the workers could memorize the material.

It was also the tradition in tobacco factories to have open discussions on the readings without interrupting the work. Workers even debated and voted on which works would be read each day. Cuban cigar workers were some of the smartest and most politically active workers in North America in the late 1800s.

until the Ten Years' War began in 1868. At that time, many Havana cigar manufacturers moved to Key West to avoid the conflict. The location was convenient for them, because the southern tip of Florida was only 90 miles (145 km) from Cuba. Making cigars in Florida also made it easier to sell cigars in the United States.

Carlos Manuel de Céspedes, son of the Cuban rebel leader, became mayor of Key West in 1875. The next year, the Spanish-language newspaper *El Yara* was founded to keep the ideals of the Cuban revolution alive. In the 1880s, Key West boasted more than 80 cigar factories employing about 3,000 workers. Fernando Figueredo and Manuel Patricio Delgado were elected from the Key West area to Florida's state assembly.

> **Fast Fact**
>
> By 1890, Key West had a population of 18,000 and seemed to be practically a province of Cuba. At that time, the city was one of the most prosperous in the state of Florida.

The Rise of Cuban Tampa

Some cigar manufacturers found themselves limited in Key West, a small island that could be reached only by ship. The shortage of skilled workers meant that cigar manufacturers had to pay high wages to the workers. The business owners did not want to do this. When the railroad reached Tampa Bay, Florida, in 1884, that city became attractive to Cuban manufacturers. Vicente Martínez Ybor, a cigar maker in Key West, bought a 49-acre (20-ha) swamp 2 miles (3.2 km) northeast of downtown Tampa in 1885 and opened a cigar-making factory. Soon, the area known as

Ybor City, and later developments in nearby West Tampa, Palmetto Beach, and Port Tampa, became centers of a thriving Spanish-language culture.

In the 1890s, several thousand Italian immigrants also moved to Ybor City. The Tampa area developed into a manufacturing port where many different races and nationalities mixed. Ybor City earned a reputation for active workers and radical politics. Like Latinos in the southwestern United States, Cuban factory owners and workers established mutual-aid societies to help the cigar-making community. By 1895, West Tampa and Ybor City together boasted 120 factories with some 5,000 workers, most of them Cuban.

Cuban immigrants in Florida reflected all social classes and skin colors. In the mid-1880s, more than 20 percent of Cuban immigrants to the United States were black or mulatto (mixed-race). Middle-class professionals, cigar workers, and business owners were all jumbled together in the same community. Many cigar manufacturers, such as Vicente Ybor, supported Cuban

Paulina Pedroso

Paulina Pedroso (1845–1925), was born in Cuba, the descendant of slaves. Paulina and her husband, Ruperto were extremely loyal supporters of Cuban independence. In the 1880s, the Pedrosos moved to Ybor City to work in the V. M. Ybor Cigar Factory and opened a boardinghouse.

José Martí often stayed with the Pedrosos when he visited Tampa in the 1890s. Once, when someone attempted to assassinate Martí by poisoning him, Paulina nursed him back to health. After that incident, Ruperto slept in the hallway outside Martí's door to prevent any more assassination attempts.

The Pedrosos sold their boardinghouse in 1905. Paulina returned to Cuba in 1910 and died there 15 years later. The Pedroso property is still owned by the Cuban government, which donated $25,000 in 1957 to complete José Martí Park. In 1993, Paulina Pedroso was inducted into the Florida Women's Hall of Fame.

independence and allowed workers to collect funds for a Cuban revolution in their factories. The Cuban revolutionaries in Florida were extremely active and powerful. Spanish general Martínez Campos complained that Tampa was "the very heart of the American conspiracy" to liberate Cuba.

In the Tampa area, black and white Cubans lived side by side. Such integration was extremely unusual, especially for a southern state in the 1890s. At that time, the U.S. government encouraged racial segregation and refused to pass laws to prevent racial violence, such as the lynching of African Americans. José Rivero Muñiz, who lived in Florida at the time, wrote, "White and Negro Cubans lived in harmony, all being admitted without exception to the various revolutionary clubs, none ever protested." Although Muñiz overstated the degree of friendship, there was some truth in his claim that the "relations between Cuban whites and Negroes were most cordial and there was no racial discrimination. . . . They were mutually respectful."

The Founding of the Cuban Revolutionary Party

José Martí made his first trip to Florida in 1891. He visited Ybor City and Tampa at the request of José Dolores Poyo, Fernando Figueredo, and other leading Cubans in Florida. Martí wanted to reach out to the Florida workers' communities and unite them with the older New York Cuban groups.

In November 1891, Martí delivered two famous speeches at the Cuban Lyceum in Tampa. Martí's speeches supporting an independent Cuba were successful beyond his wildest dreams. Members of the Cuban Patriotic League of Tampa decided to join with Martí to support a revolt against Spain. Martí used the ideas in his speeches to create two docu ments now known as the Tampa Resolutions and the Bases of the Cuban Revolutionary Party. He wanted nothing less than to unite all conflicting political, economic, and racial interests behind the dream of Cuban independence.

In January 1892, Martí founded the Cuban Revolutionary Party (also known as the PRC for its Spanish name, Partido Revolucionario Cubano). He hoped that his new PRC could unite all local Cuban patriotic organizations and social clubs. The PRC raised money in the United States and encouraged people in Cuba to rebel against the Spanish. In January 1892, Martí drafted the general organizing principles of the PRC at a political rally in Ybor City.

Martí then returned to New York City. On March 14, 1892, he published the first issue of a new Spanish-language paper called *La Patria,* the official voice of the PRC. The PRC's first goal was "to achieve with the united efforts of all men of goodwill the complete independence of the island of Cuba, and to encourage and assist with the independence of Puerto Rico."

Puerto Ricans in the United States

As the PRC's statement suggests, Puerto Ricans usually felt their fate was tied to the fate of Cuba. Cuba was larger, more heavily populated, and more valuable to Spain. It seemed logical that what happened to one would happen to the other.

Beginning in the 1820s, Puerto Ricans rebelled against the Spanish several times, but these revolts were all put down. When the Ten Years' War began in Cuba in 1868, a similar revolt, called the Lares Rebellion, broke out in Puerto Rico. The Spanish made some reforms, such as abolishing slavery in 1873, but the island remained a secure colony of Spain.

Puerto Ricans had traveled to and from the United States throughout the 19th century. For example, the 1860 census of New Haven, Connecticut, counted 10 Puerto Ricans, including Augustus Rodríguez, who later fought in the U.S. Civil War. However, Puerto Rican immigration to the United States greatly increased in the last third of the century. Hundreds of Puerto Rican immigrants, including philosopher and educator Eugenio María de Hostos, doctor and abolitionist Ramón Emeterio Betances, writer Lola Rodríguez de Tió, newspaper editor Sotero Figueroa, and historian Arturo Alfonso Schomburg, moved to New York City. By 1900, more than 1,000 Puerto Ricans lived in New York City. They created a small but thriving community with boardinghouses, small businesses, restaurants, grocery stores (bodegas), and churches.

Historian Arturo Alfonso Schomburg is shown in a photograph from 1904.

Many of these Puerto Rican immigrants supported the island's independence from Spain. In 1895, they created the

Puerto Rican Section of the PRC. Puerto Ricans, with support from Cubans, hoped the two nations would be joined together in some way when independence finally came. In 1895, there was no reason to think that the Spanish colonies of Puerto Rico and Cuba would actually take very different paths in the next century.

The United States Wins an Empire

8

In the early 1890s, José Martí traveled widely through the United States, trying to raise money for a revolution in Cuba. He organized Cuban patriotic clubs in New York and along the East Coast. He inspired crowds with his speeches. Martí sent agents into Cuba to make contact with the rebel groups on the island.

In 1894, General Máximo Gómez and Martí met in New York and created a daring plan. They arranged an invasion of Cuba by a small group of trained soldiers. The two men hoped a revolt would break out in Cuba at the same time. Martí bought three ships with PRC funds. The vessels docked at Fernandina Beach on Amelia Island in northeast Florida. At Fernandina, one of the oldest cities in Florida, the Cuban rebels loaded the boats with weapons and supplies.

This Fernandina plan had a strange result. A member of the PRC revealed the plan to one of the captains of the ships. Soon, the story spread along the Florida waterfront. The U.S. government did not want private citizens living in Florida to invade Cuba. In January 1895, the U.S. government seized the three ships loaded with weapons at Fernandina Beach. Martí escaped back to New York, but most of the men on board were arrested.

To everyone's surprise, the collapse of the Fernandina plan did not end hopes for a Cuban revolt. The failure actually inspired the revolutionary movement. The Cuban exile communities in New York and Florida rallied to the cause of *Cuba Libre,* or "a Free Cuba." Less than three weeks after the failure of the Fernandina plan, the PRC issued an order for a general revolt against Spain in Cuba. Fittingly, the order was smuggled into the island in a cigar rolled in Florida.

The Cuban Revolt began on February 24, 1895. "The news of the breakout of the revolution in Cuba," announced the *Tampa Tribune,* "has kindled the sacred flames of patriotism of every Cuban altar in the city." Huge crowds gathered in front of Florida's cigar factories to hear news of the revolution. Inside, cigar workers listened to the readers' accounts of the battles in the newspapers. One by one, the Cuban leaders in exile slipped back to the island. In April 1895, José Martí returned to Cuba for the first time in nearly 16 years. On May 19, he was killed by Spanish troops at the battle of Dos Rios.

The Cuban Revolt

Martí's death slowed down the Cuban independence movement, but it did not stop it. The Cubans continued fighting, and the rebels won some victories against Spain. By 1896, they controlled most of the Cuban countryside, while the Spanish still controlled the large cities. Spain sent more than 200,000 soldiers to Cuba but could not win the war. Cubans in New York raised money, sent weapons, and launched a propaganda war. The Spanish charged that without help from the United States, the Cuban Revolt would collapse.

In 1896, Spanish general Valeriano Weyler organized a cruel "reconcentration" policy. He tried to move the entire population of the Cuban countryside into prisonlike camps. Cubans died by the thousands in these camps, victims of unhealthy conditions, overcrowding, and disease. Weyler hoped this policy would destroy the rebellion's popular appeal. Instead, the brutality of the camps created a wave of support for the cause of Cuban independence. Newspapers in the United States filled their pages with stories of Weyler's reconcentration camps. Politicians appeared at rallies to raise money, and pro-Cuban feeling swept over much of the Midwest and West.

In 1896, the U.S. Congress passed resolutions welcoming the future independence of Cuba. Speakers attacked the Spanish so viciously that anti-U.S. riots broke out in Spain. President Grover Cleveland urged Spain to grant the island limited independence. However, the Cuban situation was not considered a crisis when William McKinley became president in 1897.

Insurgent rebel cavalry armed with machetes charges Spanish soldiers, in this drawing by Thor de Thulstrup from an American newspaper of 1896.

What Caused the *Maine* Explosion?

The actual cause of the *Maine* explosion is still unclear. A U.S. investigating board met in March 1898, before the United States declared war on Spain. It concluded that a bomb outside the ship had caused the sinking of the *Maine*. However, the board admitted that it "was unable to obtain evidence fixing responsibility . . . upon any person or persons."

Over the last hundred years, several new investigations have considered the *Maine* question. In 1976, a new study concluded that an accidental explosion inside the *Maine* probably caused the damage. In 1998, a debate among experts at the U.S. Naval Institute still could not decide if the *Maine* had been destroyed on purpose or by accident. However, no evidence has ever appeared that a Spaniard blew up the ship.

Late in 1897, a new government in Spain replaced Weyler. The government agreed to grant the Cubans and Puerto Ricans some form of limited independence. It also released political prisoners and North Americans from Cuban jails. Just when a solution seemed possible, Spanish army officers rioted against the new Spanish policy in Havana in January 1898. The riots shook President McKinley's confidence in Spain's ability to control Cuba. On January 24, he ordered a battleship, the USS *Maine*, to sail to Havana, even though the United States was not at war with Spain at the time.

"Remember the *Maine*"

At 9:40 on the evening of February 15, 1898, an explosion rocked the *Maine* in Havana's harbor. The blast killed 266 members of the ship's crew (out of 354). The actual cause of the *Maine* explosion has never been determined. Whatever the cause, war fever swept the United States.

On April 11, 1898, President McKinley asked Congress for a

declaration of war against Spain. A week later, the U.S. Congress passed a resolution recognizing the independence of Cuba and allowing the use of U.S. armed forces to drive out the Spanish. Congress passed a declaration of war on April 25, and McKinley signed it the same afternoon.

One small amendment to the declaration of war was crucial to Cuba's fate. Colorado senator Henry Teller proposed that Congress agree that the United States would not annex Cuba after the war. The Teller Amendment passed without any opposition. However, Congress said nothing about other Spanish possessions, such as Puerto Rico in the Caribbean or the Philippines in the Pacific, that the United States might want to acquire if it won the war.

The Spanish-American War

The Spanish-American War (1898) lasted only 113 days; it began in April and was over by August. By the end of the summer, Spain had been defeated by superior U.S. forces, especially at sea.

The U.S. entry into the Cuban Revolt against Spain was a huge disappointment to Cubans in Cuba and the United States. Cubans lost control of their own revolution just when they thought they had won it. The United States dealt directly with Spain during peace negotiations as though the Cuban liberation movement did not exist.

> **Fast Fact**
>
> Approximately 5,500 North Americans died in the Spanish-American War, but only 379 died in battle. The rest fell victim to a variety of accidents and diseases. Spanish and Cuban casualties are not known for sure. An estimated 50,000 Spaniards died in the war, about 90 percent from disease.

The Spanish-American War officially ended with the Treaty of Paris in December 1898. No Cuban signed this treaty—only Spanish and U.S. representatives. The treaty granted independence to Cuba and gave the Philippines, Puerto Rico, and Guam to the United States. By a narrow vote, the U.S. Senate approved the Treaty of Paris on February 6, 1899. Even though Cuba was now independent, the U.S. Army continued to occupy the country.

The *Maine* had blown up less than a year earlier, and now the United States had a colonial empire that stretched from the Caribbean to Asia. For Cubans, it was a bitter blow. General Máximo Gómez expressed the disappointment of the Cuban patriots. "None of us thought that the American intervention would be followed by a military occupation of our country by our allies, who treat us as a people incapable of acting for ourselves. . . . This cannot be our ultimate fate after years of struggle."

"Little or No Independence . . ."

José Martí had said, "Once the United States is in Cuba, who will get her out?" The United States had supposedly fought the war against Spain to free Cuba from Spanish rule. Now, the United States was not willing to let Cuba be independent.

At first, U.S. forces simply occupied independent Cuba from 1898 to 1902. The United States took over the government and the economy. Wealthy Cuban landowners regained their old positions. North American companies were given special privileges. Everything Martí had feared about the United States dominating Cuba came to pass.

In 1900, a Cuban constitutional convention met in Havana and drafted a framework for the new Cuban government. At this convention, the United States pressured the Cubans into accepting the Platt Amendment (after Senator Orville Platt of Connecticut). According to the Platt Amendment, Cuba agreed to make no treaties with other countries without U.S. approval. The amendment also permitted the United States to intervene in Cuban affairs. The Platt Amendment was placed directly into the Cuban constitution of 1901.

Cuba was also forced to agree to sell or lease lands to the United States for naval bases. In 1903, the United States leased a site in Cuba on Guantánamo Bay for a naval base that grew to cover more than 40 square miles (104 km²). The United States still controls this piece of Cuban soil.

U.S. soldiers land at El Caney, Cuba, in 1898 at the end of the Spanish–American War.

Mexican Americans and the Spanish-American War

Mexican Americans took different positions on the Spanish-American War. Some Spanish-language newspapers supported Spain. Others warned Cubans that the United States meant to take over their country.

However, once the United States declared war on Spain in 1898, most Mexican Americans seem to have rallied behind the U.S. flag. Leading Mexican-American politicians, such as Miguel Otero and Casimiro Barela, urged Latinos to support the United States in the war. Hundreds of Mexican Americans joined the army, for adventure, for money, or for Cuba Libre.

The Cubans reluctantly accepted the Platt Amendment because it seemed the only way to get the United States out of Cuba. Cubans felt that any degree of Cuban self-government was better than none at all. Although the U.S. Army left Cuba in 1902, the Platt Amendment allowed the United States to dominate Cuban politics and the economy for the next 30 years. As General Leonard Wood wrote to Theodore Roosevelt, "There is, of course, little or no independence left Cuba under the Platt Amendment."

The Spanish-American War also ended the close bonds that had linked Cubans and Puerto Ricans throughout most of the 1800s. Cuba gained a sort of independence but Puerto Rico became a colony of the United States, controlled by the U.S. government. More than 100 years later, Puerto Rico remains a colony of the United States.

U.S. Latinos in a New Century

The story of Latinos in the United States in the 1800s is mainly a story of Mexican Americans and Cuban Americans. It involves two major wars in which the United States defeated Mexico and then Spain and conquered an empire.

However, in the 1900s, the increasing prosperity of the United States and better and cheaper transportation made the country a magnet for Spanish-speaking people throughout the Western Hemisphere. Dominicans, Puerto Ricans, Salvadorans, Nicaraguans, Panamanians, Guatemalans, Colombians, and many other national groups would all immigrate to the United States in large numbers and play a major role in U.S. life in the 1900s.

In addition, the increasing power of the United States led the country to become even more involved in the Caribbean, Central America, and South America. U.S. businesses searched for raw materials, cheap labor, and people to buy their finished products. Spanish-speaking nations in the Western Hemisphere provided all three. Seeing the possibility of huge profits in the heavily populated areas of Latin America, U.S. corporations wanted to expand into these markets.

The Spanish-American War of 1898, therefore, marked the close of an era. In the next period, more Latinos would come to the United States. At the same time, the United States would take a more active role in the lives of Latinos in their home countries.

Timeline

1821	The United States takes over the Spanish colony of Florida. Mexico wins its independence from Spain.
1834	The Mexican government takes over Catholic missions in California.
1836	The Republic of Texas is established.
1845	Texas is annexed to the United States and becomes the 28th U.S. state.
1846	The Mexican American War begins.
1848	The Treaty of Guadalupe Hidalgo ends the Mexican-American War.
1849	The California gold rush begins.
1850	California becomes the 31st U.S. state.
1868	The Ten Years' War for Cuban independence begins.
1873	The *Virginius* affair brings the United States and Spain to the brink of war.
1876	Porfirio Díaz comes to power in Mexico.
1878	The Ten Years' War ends in a stalemate.
1880	José Martí arrives in New York City.
1892	The Partido Revolucionario Cubano (PRC) is founded in New York City.
1894	The Alianza Hispano Americana is founded.
1895	The Fernandina Plan to invade and liberate Cuba fails. The PRC gives the order for a general revolt in Cuba. José Martí is killed in Cuba.
1898	The United States defeats Spain in the Spanish-American War. The United States occupies Cuba and takes over Puerto Rico.
1901	The Cuban government includes the Platt Amendment in its first Constitution.

Glossary

anexionistas Cubans in the 1800s who wanted Cuba to join the United States as a state.

barrio A Latino neighborhood.

Californios Spanish-speaking people who settled in California before 1848.

corrido A type of Mexican folk ballad sung to polka, waltz, or march music.

criollos Settlers born in Latin America to Spanish parents

empresario A land agent, especially in Texas in the 1820s and 1830s.

filibuster An adventurer from the United States who invaded or tried to start revolutions in Latin American countries in the late 1700s and 1800s.

independentistas Cubans in the 1800s who wanted to rebel against Spain to create an independent republic of Cuba.

mestizo A person with both Spanish and American Indian ancestry.

mutualista A self-help society founded by Latino immigrants that offered health and life insurance, death benefits, and financial aid in times of trouble.

pueblo A town.

ranchero A ranch owner.

reconcentration A policy of Spanish general Valeriano Weyler in 1896 to move the Cuban rural population into prisonlike camps.

reformistas Cubans in the 1800s who wanted to reform the relationship between Spain and Cuba.

squatters People who occupy land illegally.

strike The organized act of stopping work in order to force an employer to improve working conditions.

vaqueros Latino cattle drivers or cowboys.

Further Reading

Books

Antón, Alex, and Roger Hernández. *Cubans in America.* New York: Kensington Books, 2002.

Catalano, Julie. *The Mexican Americans.* New York: Chelsea House, 1996.

Hoobler, Dorothy, and Thomas Hoobler. *The Cuban American Family Album.* Oxford: Oxford University Press, 1998.

—-. *The Mexican American Family Album.* Oxford: Oxford University Press, 1994.

Sherrow, Victoria. *Cuba.* Brookfield, CT: Twenty-first Century Books, 2001.

West, Alan. *José Martí: Man of Poetry, Soldier of Freedom.* Brookfield, CT: Millbrook Press, 1994.

Web Sites

The Handbook of Texas Online,
http://www.tsha.utexas.edu/handbook/online/

California's Untold Stories: Gold Rush!,
http://www.museumca.org/goldrush/

The U.S. Mexican War,
http://www.pbs.org/kera/usmexicanwar/

History of Cuba,
http://www.historyofcuba.com/cuba.htm

Bibliography

Books

Alter, Judy. *Mexican Americans.* Chanhassen, MN: Child's World, 2003.

American Presidents in World History, vols. 2 and 3. Westport, CT: Greenwood Press, 2003.

Fernández-Shaw, Carlos. *The Hispanic Presence in North America from 1492 to Today.* New York: Facts On File, 1999.

Gonzalez, Juan. *Harvest of Empire: A History of Latinos in the United States.* New York: Viking, 2000.

Sherrow, Victoria. *Cuba.* Brookfield, CT: Twenty-first Century Books, 2001.

Truett, Samuel, and Elliott Young, eds. *Continental Crossroads: Remapping U.S.-Mexico Borderlands History.* Durham, NC: Duke University Press, 2004.

Web Sites

Arellano, Anselmo F. "The Never-Ending Land Grant Struggle." La Herencia del Norte. URL: http://www.swanet.org/zarchives/gotcaliche/alldailyeditions/ 97jun/234.html. Downloaded on June 22, 2006.

Oakland Museum of California. "California's Untold Stories: Gold Rush!" URL: http://www.museumca.org/goldrush/. Downloaded on June 22, 2006.

PBS. "The U.S. Mexican War." URL: http://www.pbs.org/kera/usmexicanwar/. Downloaded on April 13, 2006.

Sanchez, Enrique. "José Julián Martí: Cuba's Greatest Hero, Poet, Statesman." URL: http://members.aol.com/josemarticuba/index1.html. Downloaded on June 22, 2006.

Index

About the Author

Matthew Kachur

Matthew Kachur holds a B.A. in journalism from New York University and a Ph.D. in American history from Queens College, CUNY Graduate Center. For 25 years, Kachur has worked as an editor and writer, notably as a supervisor for the development of *The American History Herald*, a newspaper for elementary and high school students. He also coauthored *The Slave Trade*, a book in Chelsea House's "Slavery in the Americas" series.

Jon Sterngass

Jon Sterngass's most recent books were a biography of José Martí and a history of Filipino Americans. He is also the author of *First Resorts: Pursuing Pleasure at Saratoga Springs, Newport, and Coney Island* (2001). Born in Brooklyn, New York, Sterngass has a B.A. in history and philosophy from Franklin and Marshall College, an M.A. in medieval history from the University of Wisconsin-Milwaukee, and a Ph.D. in American history from City University of New York.

Mark Overmyer-Velázquez

Mark Overmyer-Velázquez, general editor and author of the preface included in each of the volumes, holds a B.A. in History and German Literature from the University of British Columbia, and an M.A., M.Phil., and Ph.D.s in Latin American and Latino History from Yale University. While working on a new book project on the history of Mexican migration to the United States, he teaches undergraduate and graduate courses in Latin American and U.S. Latina/o history at the University of Connecticut.